Praise

'Personal, credible, practical. ____ ___ ___.
behaviour change. A powerful read.'
— **Sir John Timpson CBE**, Chairman, Timpson

'Grab the magic from Ruth and her network of
conscious leaders.'
— **Andy Woodfield**, PwC Partner and Author

'Highly recommended read for any leader with a
heart for their people and a mind for business success
and sustainability.'
— **Hephzi Pemberton**, CEO, The Equality Group

'Fantastic, practical read – this book is filled with
real-life examples. They allow you to not only
understand the concepts, but how to implement
them.'
— **Rosie Anderson**, Associate Director,
    Accenture

'Insightful, readable and inspiring.'
— **Mark Reynolds**, CEO, Hable Group

'Smart yet simple success stories to inspire, from
people who love their people.'
— **June Cory**, Founder, MyMustard

'*Next Level Leadership* brings the best of many concepts together in one read. Every person who reads the book will find themselves in it and will find something new to help them on their leadership journey.'
— **Annette Jensen**, Organisational Effectiveness Lead, Humana

'Wise, compassionate, successful leadership for today – get your notebook ready!'
— **Ciaron Dunne**, CEO, Genie Ventures

'A fresh look at leadership from a wide range of people facing different challenges – very inspiring.'
— **Ann Hawkins**, Mentor and Business Advisor, Drive, the Collaborative Network

'Ruth captures the necessity, nuance and challenge of conscious leadership.'
— **Matt Thompsett**, CVO, Green Lemon Company

Next Level Leadership

Nine Lessons from Conscious Leaders

RUTH FARENGA

Rethink

First published in Great Britain in 2022
by Rethink Press (www.rethinkpress.com)

Cover image © Tom Benford at WONGDOODY

Headphones icon created by Adrien Coquet from
NounProject.com

Leaf icon created by St Musdalifah from NounProject.com

Contents

Introduction

I could give you all the 'worky' reasons why I wrote this book. The reality is that starting the Conscious Leaders Podcast and writing *Next Level Leadership* is the culmination of a journey.

Some years ago I experienced a toxic situation at work that made me doubt myself, resulted in crippling anxiety and ended with handing in my resignation. I began to see a career coach and soon realised that where previously I had been made to feel worthless, by way of looks and insinuation, now I began to feel accepted, capable and empowered through the inter-actions with my coach.

It was only years later that I started to digest this con-trasting experience more fully. Why is it that around some people we feel lacking in self-esteem or disempowered, and with others, we feel amazing, as though we could conquer the world? If only we could find the reasons, we could tap into a leadership superpower.

This is what motivated me to start a business, interview leaders and write this book, with one goal in mind: I want to serve your development as a leader.

For you to have picked up this book, you must care a lot about people. You likely have ideas and aspirations for yourself and others, want to effect real change and take your leadership to the next level. In that endeavour, you may also want to support others in a way that helps them get over their hurdles so they can grow and develop more fully.

An understanding of great leadership traits will help you make significant changes quickly to support your own and others' ambitions.

Throughout this book, I will be sharing the top 'lessons' I have observed from the three years I've spent interviewing leaders for the Conscious Leaders Podcast. These lessons are traits and behaviours that are common among the leaders.

This book will introduce you to these leaders. You will discover what goes through their minds on a philosophical and practical level. I have drawn out the commonalities – what they have worked on and how they practise it.

I hope that reading this book allows you to pause and reflect on how you spend your time as a leader, what kind of environment you create and how you show up for others. Wherever you are on your leadership journey, this book will facilitate your ability to do your best work.

PART ONE
THE CONTEXT FOR CONSCIOUS LEADERS

This first part of the book will set the scene. For us to move on to unpacking great leadership traits, we need to understand human behaviour. This is a vast topic, but I have pulled out some of the key points from both a personal level and a systemic level. We then see the context for employees as we seek to help them reach their potential.

1
Setting the scene

I carried out research back in autumn 2019 and I found that leaders like learning from other leaders.[1] They want to know what's working and how that plays out practically so they can tweak it and try it out for themselves. By leaders, I refer mainly to CEOs and founders as well as others at a senior level. I hope wherever you are on your leadership journey, this book will facilitate your ability to do your best work.

My other motivation is that, like many, I feel I have experienced some of the best and worst of leadership in organisations. I have noticed throughout my career the ability of my manager to influence my capacity and outlook on the world. At times, I felt the world was my oyster and at others, weak, scared and lost.

The evidence is there from research. A 2017 Gallup study of more than 1 million people in the US reported that 75% left their job because of their manager and not the position itself.[2] This supports the well-known adage that 'employees join companies but leave managers'.

On the positive side, among the clients I coach I have witnessed many leaders' capacity to make personal changes that create huge positive ripples in other people's behaviour and the wider company culture. This transforms the capacity of the organisation to have impact and its people enjoy the journey. This doesn't mean things are always smooth sailing; it is about development and growth and connecting more as human beings so we can bring our full selves to our lives as well as possible.

You may have heard of Kintsugi, the Japanese technique of repairing pottery with a golden glue. By embracing the flaws, the repairers create something stronger and more beautiful than the original. There is, of course, a message for us about life here: we can become stronger through adversity.

This was certainly true for me. It was my darkest moments at work that led me to train to teach mindfulness-based cognitive therapy (MBCT), qualify as a professional coach and create my business, Conscious Leaders, and the Conscious Leaders Podcast. The podcast was set up to help showcase the best leaders I could find. These leaders are incredible, but they are also regular human beings with normal trials in their lives. They have found inspiration and motivation to change their behaviour, the behaviour of others and the wider impact they have. I have sought to hack into their thoughts and delve into the depths of their consciousness so we can all gain the fruits of what they have learnt.

Conscious leadership

You may ask, 'What does conscious leadership really mean?' In this context, it is the extent to which a leader has stepped up for their people – the extent to which they are pushing boundaries and doing more radical or innovative things in the way they lead to help their people go further. They are not satisfied with an average kind of leadership; they care, want to inspire and motivate more than most I have seen. They are prepared to work on themselves and make sacrifices to achieve that.

A lot of professional development training I observe is caught up in techniques and models. These can be useful, but the first step we need to address is how we embark (or continue) on our personal development journey. As the pioneer of contemporary leadership research, Warren Bennis, famously said, '... the process of becoming a leader is much the same as the process of becoming an integrated human being'.[3]

For me, this is an ongoing journey. It is a life's work, but I will endeavour to keep it practical. It takes conscious step-by-step work to be centred enough to support ourselves and others. I will call on academic theory, and my own experience and training as a coach, so you get rounded professional development as part of this book.

I often say to people in workshops and one-to-one coaching that I am not the finished product. I'm not claiming to have reached some kind of enlightenment. I am still working on myself each day through meditation, refection and how I relate to and build a strong culture around those I work with. There was a time when I was all too earnest with this work. It is key that we don't put pressure on ourselves, but engage in our self-development lightly.

I frequently ask myself, 'How can I live my life with more ease and fun?' Throughout this book, I want to demonstrate the significance of my work, but I also want you to enjoy it. We can all take ourselves too seriously sometimes; we will have more energy and resources if we release our foot from the accelerator pedal and enjoy the journey as well as we can.

While you are reading this book, I encourage you to take pauses. Leaders are often working at pace in adrenaline-fuelled ways. That adrenaline can be addictive, so I hope this book represents an opportunity for you to consider your own wellbeing and slow down, giving yourself time to think and reflect. I have included this leaf icon before the key takeaways and pointers at the end of each lesson to prompt you to do so if you choose.

During your pause, you may like to take in a deep breath and slowly exhale a few times before you continue reading.

Sustainability and performance at the centre

In this book, I start by exploring the reasons why people are the way they are. This is important because it sets the fundamental context of both human behaviour and current workforce trends so that we can navigate this environment from the right starting point.

The leaders who form a key part of this book are commercially astute individuals. They are all CEOs or founders of thriving, profitable businesses who recognise that great employee engagement and retention makes their business sustainable.

Too often, we as leaders think of sustainability in an operational and tactical sense. We consider how a business should, for example, change its packaging or plant some trees. Here, I am advocating a holistic approach to sustainability that starts with how we treat people and support their wellbeing and overall performance at work.

I hope that you will see how the traits and behaviours of the leaders who have contributed to this book show their commitment to and support of their employees' wellbeing as well as the bottom line of the business. Kindness, for example, benefits the bottom line as much as it does people, so don't shy away from this. The commercial viability, success and sustainability of your organisation are vital, but they must be aligned to the wellbeing and productivity of your employees.

I frequently tell leaders that work on themselves is not 'nice to have'; it's essential and urgent. If we can sort out our own baggage, we will be in a much stronger position to support others and the business. It is a bit like rowing a boat – if we can become aligned with our people so we all row together, we will go far, but if someone is half out of the boat or rowing in the wrong direction or just plain distracted, our progress will be hindered.

Your people *are* the business. If they are strong and committed, your business will be too.

2
People are complex

It is true that people – all of us – create some drama at work, but the level of this drama is on a spectrum. Some of us create light rain showers; others create giant tornadoes of disruption.

I want to start from an agreed point of zero blame. We are largely a product of our experience. Some people have had cosy upbringings with all the love and support they could hope for. Others have had tough starts without many of their basic needs being met from an early age. These people have often had to work hard just to feel whole.

Anyone who carries issues from their upbringing into adulthood – issues caused by anything from unintended emotional manipulation to major childhood trauma – can be (even mildly) manipulative, gossipy, disruptive or destructive. Most of these issues have been born from the things they observed or encountered in social situations.

Replaying the school playground

I come from a pretty average family. My dad had a working-class upbringing, my mum's was middle class, but they both love me deeply and I have been fortunate. I was cared for as a child and encouraged to do well without ever feeling pressured, for which I'm grateful.

My mum worries a lot and is generally quite anxious. My dad, on the other hand, is less anxious, yet has experienced bouts of depression for many years. My parents argued regularly throughout my upbringing; although there was no violence towards each other, things did get smashed in anger. Perhaps because of this, I have always sought harmony in social situations. It's not surprising that I find myself in a career which helps leaders develop themselves and get along more effectively with others. I'm here to create ease and balance.

I was bullied at school; not badly, but I was at the lower end of the pecking order of popularity. I was one of the brighter ones and the teachers noticed that I was doing well, so the bullies sought to notice it too, for the wrong reasons. There would often be a large public celebration if I got something wrong and I was occasionally shoved up against a locker and threatened for reasons I didn't understand. I was probably not playing the social game in the right way. As an only child, I may not have been the greatest at knowing my place.

Kids are cruel; families can be complicated. Everyone has their own story – many have had it much worse than I did. I have shared my experience merely to state that we all come from different backgrounds. I do feel privileged for lots of reasons. My parents are amazing and I love them and treasure their strengths while forgiving them for their weaknesses. Hopefully they forgive me for mine too.

Recognising our own starting point is key here, however our past has played out. In the workplace, we are often unconsciously repeating habits and patterns from our schooldays and family situations. This behaviour can also pop up when we are under pressure, personally or professionally. If we're not aware of or dealing with these patterns, they can return over and over again.

Low self-esteem

Most habits and patterns of behaviour from our childhood are born from self-preservation and survival.

For some of us, school was about getting through the day in one piece without sticking out too much, shining too brightly or saying the wrong thing. As a result, we have learnt to be 'small' and may have developed varying amounts of low self-esteem.

The ramifications of this low self-esteem also vary in size. One client – let's call her Anne – was referred to me in my early days as a coach. Anne had the worst self-esteem issues I have ever seen; she had clearly had a tough ride in life and I felt like she doubted my intention. As a new coach, I was somewhat unseated by her behaviour.

She was sensitive to our surroundings, so we found a quiet spot for our coaching session in the café at the British Library. Unfortunately, something annoyed her before we even started, and once she got going, she unleashed a tirade of complicated information about the latest drama in her office. Interestingly, she was highly competent at her job, but found office culture challenging and certain characters incredibly difficult to work with.

I picked up on the pain she must have experienced in her past. She had been pulled in many directions emotionally, so I stayed as steady as I could to support her as she shared her experience. I coached her around mindfulness and she was surprisingly receptive, becoming proactive in her meditation practice. At other times, she disputed the coaching methods

I offered and I would remind her that she was responsible for using the time we had together wisely. She needed strong boundaries.

I have no idea about Anne's childhood, but I would guess that she didn't have strong boundaries at home, or perhaps they were unpredictable, movable, even dangerous. Her pain shone through to me and despite her challenging behaviour, I had compassion. I saw how her history was playing out in her behaviour and I wanted to support her.

More on Anne later.

Anne is an extreme example, but most workplaces have many lesser versions. Some have small niggles rumbling in the background and others have huge amounts of toxicity overflowing from the (virtual or physical) rooftops.

The issue with low self-esteem, particularly when it is unconscious, is that it leads us to find ways to artificially boost it. Sadly, this can sometimes be at the expense of others, which is often why cliques form and gossip spreads. In some workplaces, people end up feeling like they have to cover their back or keep their guard up to protect themselves. These are often the realities of people and culture.

Leaders come in all shapes and sizes, so some may be completely unaware of what is really going on among their teams. In my experience, such leaders tend to think that their workplace is a pleasant environment. They don't see the rumours, the gossip and the toxicity; they don't realise that it is actually a political and difficult place for many.

Other leaders are more tuned in and see the cracks; the gossip and clashes of personality; the nasty traits in some of their colleagues; the people who rub up against each other negatively. They realise how this gets in the way of productivity and strong relationships and want it to change. If you fall into this category, you're likely to want to support your employees' development so that you can all focus on doing your best work.

Of course, there are tons of amazing companies with fun and co-supportive cultures – perhaps you are already experiencing good progress with yours. The leaders in these companies have worked hard to establish and protect the type of environment they want; they will still be working at it now. In this book, I will give lots of examples of places where the culture is thriving. I will share both the philosophy of the leaders and how this plays out practically day to day. I've probed my contributors on what's hard and what went wrong too, so you can see the *human* side of their experience and how they have overcome obstacles. Seeing how people got through the tough stuff provides the strongest learning points.

Of course, not all employment situations are successful. Sometimes there will be a complete mismatch of values between the company and the employee. Perhaps the employee is not showing the willingness to change their attitude, so we don't want to waste huge volumes of energy to make little to no progress. At times, the best course of action is to encourage the employee to move on to a workplace better suited to their needs, but we mustn't be too quick to judge. The lessons in this book will give you an opportunity to see when radical behaviour change is possible with a bit of commitment.

It is important to understand that in dealing with difficult situations, you are doing your best work. You are role modelling, learning. You are helping people grow.

People bring their whole selves to work

It is vital to remember this. People bring whatever is going on in their personal life through the physical or virtual office door or screen.

Business owner June Cory, my second guest on the Conscious Leaders Podcast, emphasises this point. In her interview, she shares a moment when she and a few of her employees were all going through a tough time. They stood in a circle and shared their circumstances with each other.

'I was going through chemotherapy at the time,' she recounts. 'Another member of staff had an ill parent, one had a disenfranchised child and one was saving hard for a mortgage that they couldn't afford. You don't leave that at the door; you bring that into work with you, but it's OK to talk about how you're feeling.'

This is recognition from a senior leader that we are all human beings. At this moment, all these employees realised that they were connected. They were suffering, which is something we all experience as human beings. When we are connected with others in our suffering, the common humanity is powerful.

Another former leader in banking technology – let's call her Jocelyn – reported that one of her managers was going through the most horrendous time with his divorce. He was blindsided by the announcement from his wife on Christmas Eve that their marriage was over, floored by the thought of not being with the woman he adored and their children every day. As a result, he was feeling suicidal.

Jocelyn reassured him that there was absolutely no shame in him taking time off or long lunch breaks for some air or to sort out admin, or working from home. She was steadfast in her support as she sought to protect him, setting her role as company leader aside and putting him as a person at the forefront of her focus. This he found particularly helpful. Work became therapeutic, enabling him to do as little or as much as he could at any one time. Jocelyn told me his work didn't suffer, which she put down to her giving him the space to recover.

Another staff member Jocelyn supported had an alcoholic father and a volatile boyfriend. She would often spend the first thirty minutes of the day talking through her staff member's latest struggles. Had Jocelyn not given her this time, it would have been impossible for her to focus, but after she had unloaded, she was able to start her work.

This was an essential part of Jocelyn's leadership role: letting her colleague express how she was doing to enable her to extract herself from a toxic relationship. In doing so day after day during a tough period in this staff member's life, Jocelyn showed how committed she was to her as a person. Business is built on relationships and Jocelyn demonstrated her commitment to their relationship through this level of support.

I'm not saying that everyone has a full thirty minutes every day to dedicate to talking employees through their problems, but we can all lead in a way that takes into account the whole person. In Jocelyn's example, the investment of time she made in her relationship with this staff member was paid back by her commitment to Jocelyn and the firm. She moved up through the ranks from a junior level to become senior vice president within eight years: an amazing trajectory which demonstrates the power of support.

We cannot deny that people bring divorce, lost loved ones, financial insecurities and any other problems that may be dominating their lives to their day-to-day interactions in the workplace. Even if they don't talk about their problem, it's there in their psyche, affecting them and the way they perform and interact. When we as leaders recognise that and offer our people an outlet for their worries, a helping hand in dealing with whatever is getting them down and a feeling of connection so they know they're not alone, we and our companies and organisations reap the rewards in terms of committed and loyal employees. We can't put a monetary value on that.

3
How drama affects the bottom line

Drama in your business – otherwise known as the people issues – is a bottom-line conversation as much as it is one about wellbeing. People's wellbeing directly affects their ability to be productive, which directly affects the bottom line of a business.

I have always been bemused as to why any leader would think of wellbeing as a side project. They often delegate it to a junior member of staff to organise a few activities to boost wellbeing among the employees rather than integrating it into the overall employee strategy. Mindfulness-related training for leaders may come with good intention, but without follow up, it can appear to be merely a tick-box exercise for 'wellbeing week' or 'mental-health day'. Instead, it should be regarded as something that will transform wellbeing and productivity.

Wellbeing is not a side issue in your business; it concerns how your employees feel at work, and how they feel affects their motivation, commitment and day-to-day productivity. It's about leadership and culture and how you create an environment of performance which is conducive to your people's health. Wellbeing can be boosted by a number of things, including how a line manager treats their team on a daily basis; how connected team members feel to their colleagues; how proud and purposeful they feel; how much control they have over their work; and the opportunities they have to get good at things.

You may have heard of Dan Pink's autonomy, mastery and purpose as motivation factors.[4] He explores how being self-directed (autonomy), getting better at things that matter through feedback (mastery) and knowing *why* you are doing something (purpose) are the centre of motivation, debunking the 'if... then' type rewards. He has found these are only useful in the short term and don't last in terms of motivation.

This is why pay increases (above a certain level) have little impact on someone's long-term motivation. One of my podcast guests, Guy Singh-Watson, founder of UK-wide organic fruit and vegetable business, Riverford, knows that we waste a huge amount of employees' potential when we assume they are motivated by money.[5] Actually, they want to do good in the world. They want to have an impact and be treated well along the way. Wellbeing is far more motivating than money, which is why we need to talk about it in the same sentence as culture and leadership.

It really annoys me when someone reports they have 'covered' wellbeing with a few mental-health first-aiders or the odd one-off wellbeing session. For those of you unfamiliar with the term, the intention with mental-health first-aiders is that people with problems go to them as a first line of support. I'm not denying this could be a useful tactic with the right strategy behind it, but more often than not, company leaders give little thought as to whether anyone would actually want to talk to these first-aiders.

Primarily, we need to support the ability of all people, especially managers, to engage and help our employees. This is about our day-to-day conversations. Translating this into practice involves three layers of professional and personal development which, in turn, interweave into nine lessons. These three layers are self, interrelational and wider culture development.

Let me break this down. You need to start with working on yourself: your habits and behaviours. This is the same with any change – it starts with you.

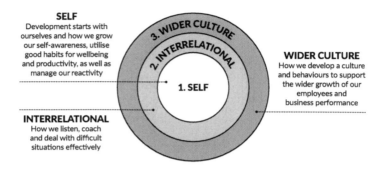

SELF
Development starts with ourselves and how we grow our self-awareness, utilise good habits for wellbeing and productivity, as well as manage our reactivity

WIDER CULTURE
How we develop a culture and behaviours to support the wider growth of our employees and business performance

INTERRELATIONAL
How we listen, coach and deal with difficult situations effectively

Secondly, the way you relate to others around you is vital. You can build your listening and coaching skills to understand what's going on and help people find the answers to drive the business forward.

Finally, the wider culture – what type of environment do you want to create? How do you make work feel motivating and enjoyable? With these three elements in co-operation, great transformational change is possible.

The cost of poor retention

The bottom-line effects of drama within your business can be seen most clearly in a lack of employee retention, which often leads to poor employee morale and low productivity. Studies predict that every time a business replaces a salaried employee, the cost on average is six to nine months' salary.[6] For a manager making £60,000, this equates to £30–45k in recruiting and training expenses.

Every time we lose a staff member, we lose all the investment we have put into them in terms of training. It also creates friction in the workplace as others may be disrupted by their departure. At worst, it can cause a mass exodus.

This doesn't mean you should hang on to people at all costs. If you lead or own a small business, you may well be aware of the limitations for future growth for your employees and realise it is only natural that they will eventually move on. That said, you want them to be committed and purposeful while they're with you, and that all comes down to wellbeing.

Simply put, contented employees tend to be loyal, productive and innovative. Discontented employees tend to cause dramas, impacting productivity, innovation and loyalty, and ultimately damaging your business's bottom line. Wellbeing is that important, so if you're not already doing so, it's time to prioritise it.

4
The changing needs of employees

A huge contextual consideration we have as leaders is the changing needs of people. This is largely driven by young people being vocal about their needs, but is becoming pervasive across the generations as others seek more balance and purpose in life in general. A great contact and friend of mine in the organisational development space, Annette Jensen, says, 'Millennials say what the baby boomers thought all along.'[7]

According to the Chartered Institute of Professional Development (CIPD) in the UK, there is something in the modern workplace called the psychological contract which 'refers to individuals' expectations, beliefs, ambitions and obligations, as perceived by the employer and the worker'.[8] It goes beyond any written contract and includes things like how people expect their manager to treat them, what ability they have to be flexible with their time and the amount of autonomy they are given. The CIPD goes on to say that the psychological contract 'provides a powerful rationale for employers to pay attention to the "human" side of the employment relationship'.

Young people have a strong need for meaning and purpose at work. One of my main clients, technology company Hable, reports a major upswing in people proactively contacting it for employment opportunities. Former managing director, Sean O'Shea, believes this is due to the company's proactive approach to wellbeing.[9] Practically, this involves wellbeing days, frequent walking meetings, regular coaching sessions as well as a keen focus on work–life balance. Sean believes this is what young people want and it's already saving the company recruitment costs as capable prospective recruits are seeking it out rather than vice versa.

The employer brand

What the Hable example shows is this company's employer brand. In competitive markets for talent such as technology, companies need to be particularly aware of this. What do people say about your company's employer brand?

What exactly is the employer brand? It is the vibe that a company provides as an employer, the culture and the perception of its purpose. How does the company live its ethos? Cultivating a powerful employer brand is essential for attracting and retaining great employees.

In conversation with me, Hable's CEO, Mark Reynolds, shared how part of the company's success is due to the down-to-earth nature of the leaders' communications.[10] Both Mark and Sean bring a lot of humour into their work – it's what the company stands for – and this is attractive to people. People can see through a polished veneer, so the leaders at Hable really embody the type of behaviour they want to see in others. There aren't any big egos there. Employees feel the vibe of groundedness and honesty and it's easily reflected throughout their behaviours and communications because it's authentic.

Company leaders need to decide what kind of employer they want to be. This means they need to know what their company stands for, be clear on the values they represent as an employer and demonstrate them in day-to-day practices and policies.

A culture consultant I work with, Laura Lewis, who runs Culture Chameleon, says:

'All too often I see organisations defining their values and thinking, "Job done", but unless the values are consciously threaded through every single moment that matters to your team and your customers, they become, in essence, nothing more than a pretty picture on the wall or your website. When you live and breathe the values in all you do as an organisation – that's when they become truly powerful. Creating values is a journey, not an event. It takes time, dedication and practice to truly bring them to life.'[11]

If there are contradictions between the values that the company preaches and the practices its leaders undertake, this undoes all the good work that the values intended.

The COVID-19 pandemic brought into sharp focus the companies that kept to their values and built on their employer brand and those that (without wanting to sound too dramatic) destroyed it. The National Trust, for example, stepped up for the UK public by leaving most of its gardens open for free in the early stages of the pandemic.

In March 2020, the director general of the National Trust said:

'We want to honour our mission – to enable people and nature to thrive. Over the coming weeks we will do all that we can to keep on providing public benefit through caring for places and giving people access wherever possible.'[12]

The National Trust could have taken a more conservative approach, but it has a value of 'inspiring people' and lived up to this, even at a difficult time.

On a global scale, Facebook (now Meta) has come up numerous times as a brand not living its values. Yes, it is a 'move fast and break things' organisation, which it certainly does live up to, but Mark Zuckerberg also talks about 'delivering happiness' and offering 'social value'. Meanwhile, Facebook is frequently in the news for not clamping down hard enough on extremist groups who use its platform to serve their own dangerous causes. Facebook facilitates both good and bad community and, despite its words, often doesn't take responsibility for the huge role it has in society.

Research on the talent market shows that graduates and professionals want to work for employers with great reputations.[13] Indeed, many thinkers in people development and human resources talk of creating a unique value proposition (UVP) as an employer that not only attracts people to the workplace, but makes them want to stay. This is all about the growth of a brand and its value, which is determined by what others say about it.

How do leaders progress in their personal and professional development to create better cultures?

How can they be better leaders so they can promote environments where people and businesses thrive? Where people have great things to say about their employer? It's tough, isn't it? Leaders are often busy people.

These questions, coupled with the time constraints on leaders, were motivation for me to research what is most effective in terms of leaders' development.

Leaders like learning from other leaders

This was the overarching takeaway from some primary research I undertook with seventy-nine business leaders in autumn 2019.[14] I wanted to find out about how much leaders understood and valued emotional intelligence (EQ), by which I mean their personal development – how they manage themselves and interrelate.

From the research, I learnt a lot about leaders, their interest in soft-skill development and the things that hold them back. Three out of four leaders said they considered EQ professional development to be valuable or extremely valuable, although others felt they didn't know enough about it at that stage, but only one in five said they made time for professional leadership development. Lack of time, 68% reported, was the biggest barrier to professional development, so it was often left at the bottom of the pile.

The clearest conclusion from my research is that leaders like informal ways to learn from their peers. They want to undertake learning in their own time and in peer groups so they can share ideas and views to come to an understanding about what's working.

From here, I set up the Conscious Leaders Podcast to unearth the best leaders I could find. Ones who really step up for their employees and are prepared to push boundaries because they care about the welfare of their teams. In doing so, I would allow other leaders to learn from them.

In the early days of the podcast, it became clear to me that I needed these leaders to open up. I wanted them to share the lows as much as the highs. It was powerful when a leader talked about how they had failed or suffered in some way and it led them to behave differently. These examples demonstrate their growth.

I interviewed the founder of Riverford, Guy Singh-Watson.[15] As the UK's largest fruit and veg box delivery company, Riverford is interesting for many reasons – my primary one being that it has moved to an employee-owned model.

What Guy revealed in his interview was his own journey. His background was in the City of London, making lots of money and managing people – something he was good at, but ultimately, he found the work soulless, so he returned to his roots in farming to develop an organic veg business. His ethical drive continued and he wanted to run Riverford in the most effective people-centred way, so he became interested in employees taking responsibility and ownership of the company. He had no desire to become richer; he wanted to do great work and be as useful to society as possible.

When Riverford employed a coach to investigate employee opinions about the business, Guy initially thought that the people issues centred around the middle management. Instead, he discovered that *he* was the biggest issue.

He went on to say that at times, his behaviour 'could be seen as bullying... and other directors started behaving in this way too'. Many employees thought the top team and the board were 'jerks' who were disengaged with what was going on with employees.

From here, Guy took radical action to review his own behaviour and work with a coach to develop himself. He was surprised how much he enjoyed it and how quickly he changed. For example, if he made a mistake going forward, he learnt to recognise it and apologise swiftly and publicly.

In my experience, real change starts at the top. Grassroots change is possible, but only when the leadership is willing to listen, self-aware enough to recognise their own faults and prepared to act on feedback. Guy's action exemplifies conscious leadership – he woke up to the change that his employ-ees wanted to see in him, listened and acted on it.

He didn't just listen once; he set up a company partly run by co-owner councils ('co-owners' is Riverford's term for employees) that are elected and continu-ally drive change through the evolving opinions of employees. In other words, he set about changing the whole infrastructure and decision making of the com-pany. That change started with him.

In the interviews I have conducted for the podcast, I have sought to draw out both the high-level philoso-phy of the guests and how it plays out practically day to day. I am a strong believer in change, but to make change happen, we need practical solutions. To make those solutions happen, we often need to develop hab-its that make it easy for us to implement the change we want over the long term.

Someone who speaks eloquently on this subject is Professor Paul Dolan, behavioural scientist at London School of Economics.[16] He talks about the fact that the vast majority of our thinking is driven by our uncon-scious and the stories we've been telling ourselves. By 'stories', he means patterns that have often been on repeat for weeks, months, years or decades.

This means that we don't think consciously about our decision making. We may think we are making con-scious choices when, in fact, we are not. Instead, we are driven by our experience, which is all related to us largely being a product of our conditioning. When it's left unattended, this means we are often playing out habits and behaviours learnt in our family and school playground interactions.

Professor Dolan talks about 'happiness by design', which means designing our environment in a way that is conducive to change. This could be as simple as having an end-of-week reflection time where we spend fifteen minutes looking out of the window, reviewing what has gone well in that week. As a rule, one of my podcast guests, Bejay Mulenga, does not take meetings before 10am. This gives him time to clear his head and concentrate on his own wellbeing and intentions for the day and resource himself before he resources others.

I hope that by learning how other leaders are progressing their skills, you will be able to apply the ones that resonate most with you to your own life and work. You may like to think about what else would support you in this endeavour, such as associating with other leaders on a similar journey. From what I have seen, conscious leadership is infectious.

Your role as a leader

This work is about how you behave, how you dedicate your time and the environment you want to build. Clearly, time is finite, so it is crucial to think about the way you use your time effectively, including in the way you behave.

Groundbreaking global research by Daniel Goleman has shown that a leader's soft skill or EQ is much more relevant than their cognitive skill or IQ.[17] Goleman has evolved his model on EQ to be specific about the soft skills that he observes in successful leaders.

He defines EQ through four key areas: self-awareness, self-management, social awareness and relationship management. The more that you as a leader manage each of these areas, the higher your EQ.

The *Harvard Business Review* has gone so far as to say EQ is 'a ground-breaking, paradigm-shattering idea'.[18] Goleman found direct ties between EQ in leaders and measurable business results. He studied competency models (competencies of leaders) and analysed data from over 188 companies (mainly large corporates) to determine which of the leaders' 'personal capabilities really drove performance' in their particular companies and teams.[19] He discovered that EQ was critical for those in the senior ranks of an organisation. Nearly 90% of the differences that leaders of high-performance departments had were attributable to EQ factors over IQ.

EQ will become even more important in the future than it is today. Good business leaders rely on their staff, and these people need leaders and an organisational culture that encourages them to be the best they can be. This means that leaders largely need to stay out of the technical side of the business, the detail, and concentrate on the relational.

The lessons from this research are about building a leader's EQ, but they are actually much more practical. What I'm seeking to do in this book is make them as tangible and relevant to you as possible.

Activist for civil and children's rights Marian Wright Edelman says, 'You can't be what you can't see.'[20] This applies perfectly to making a change as a leader. You need to picture how you want to behave to be able to make it happen. The content of this book will enable you to learn the traits and behaviours of successful leaders so that you can adopt them if you choose. All of these are practices, which means, like most things in life, they take work, but change can happen rapidly when your intention to work on yourself is strong.

PART TWO
NINE LESSONS FROM CONSCIOUS LEADERS

Your commitment to work on yourself as a leader is the first step towards change. By turning inwards to look at your own behaviours and habits, you will have much more outward impact.

I've narrowed the lessons I've learnt from conscious leaders down to nine traits and behaviours. These will allow you a chance to work on yourself in a way that transforms you and others.

5
Lesson 1: Develop
a clear intention

The best leaders I have found demonstrate a clear intention. By this, I mean they are pure about their attitude towards people and firm on their beliefs and values. They are not clouded or jaded – they are strong and this attitude comes from a place of good ethics.

Clear intention is shown through a leader's deep care for their employees alongside their will to challenge them to grow, both as people and part of the fulfilment of the purpose of the company.

Put simply, if leaders nurture employees, the employees will help fulfil that purpose.

CASE STUDY: COMPASSION AND HAPPINESS

EPISODE 10: THE CONSCIOUS LEADERS PODCAST

A great example of strong and clear intention comes from a guest I interviewed called Pip Jamieson. Pip is founder and CEO of The Dots, 'the LinkedIn for creatives' as reported by *Forbes*.[21] Pip has the most compassionate approach I have ever seen in a leader. She cares deeply about her employees' wellbeing and takes practical moves to demonstrate this.

One of the ways she does this is a simple survey every quarter – a 'temperature check' on how employees are feeling. Her first question is 'How happy do you feel at work out of ten?' If the answer is under seven, she invites people to book a meeting with her to see if she can help in some way.

Pip leans into employees talking to her about their personal and professional needs, and is open with hers, too. She recently went through the process of freezing her eggs, so shared how this was for her. She also asks employees what they would do if they were the CEO to glean insights from them about the strategic direction of the company – something she has sought to improve iteratively since the company's conception.

Feedback from employees comprises of anything from improving the office chairs to the way they would structure group meetings, to wider opinions on the culture or overall business direction. She says she wants their input and she means it.

She's keen that employees connect with and support each other. The company has a system which pairs employees with a new colleague each week to have a virtual 'coffee chat'. Zero work agenda, just time for new recruits to get to know another individual within the company.

A third way she shows her concern for employees' wellbeing is through her understanding of the value of a simple thank you. Consequently, employees have a weekly meeting called 'Thank you Fridays' where they are able to recognise and celebrate great things that their colleagues have done. These things may be small or simple, but cumulatively they create a culture of appreciation.

What Pip shows in great measure is the ability to create systems and habits that stick, thereby embodying her desire to care for her employees. Pip ensures that her philosophy embeds itself into as many touchpoints as it can within her organisation, so her employer brand and values waterfall throughout the teams. Her intention shines through practically. Be under no illusion, though; Pip has worked at this. She's continually listening to feedback from employees.

Many employees report that their bosses are out of touch, somewhere disconnected in virtual or physical ivory towers. Pip is the opposite. She's really connected.

As part of my interview with Pip, I asked her if she ever felt drained by other people sharing their problems and personal lives with her. She said she doesn't; she is keen to listen and for them to share. She has the most boundless amount of compassion that I have ever seen.

Strong and clear intentions

The value of a strong and clear intention shows up when we are dealing with difficult situations. In this way, the equity of our intention will build up and pay dividends later.

Clear intentions are pure – they are not clouded. The best way to explain this is with an example. If you want to give someone at your company feedback to help them change their behaviour, but really you think they are not cut out for the job and can't change, your intention will be clouded by your doubt about them. Despite your words of feedback and encouragement, they will know that you don't have their best intentions at heart. They will feel it.

As human beings, we are wired to receive communication in lots of ways. If we're saying one thing while thinking something different, other people will know. This may not be a conscious knowing, but it will be communicated.

CASE STUDY: DIRECT AND MEANINGFUL COMMUNICATION

EPISODE 6: THE CONSCIOUS LEADERS PODCAST

The best example I have of this from the podcast comes from Andy Woodfield, who is a Partner at PwC. When I first met Andy, I was struck by how open he was with me. It was just after the first lockdown ended in July 2020 that I went to his house in Poole to interview him. I immediately felt like I knew him, which was quite a strange feeling to have. It points to how open Andy is as an individual and a leader.

In his interview, he was candid. This is one of Andy's strengths: he tells it how it is. He explained how he once gave one of his senior managers some direct feedback after hearing reports that this particular person was behaving terribly towards others. She was being rude and treating people badly, which was out of character.

He decided this behaviour needed nipping in the bud as quickly as possible, so he spoke to her about it.

'I said to her directly, "People have been telling me you're behaving super nasty",' Andy told me. '"I'm wondering what's going on because I know that you're not like that."' Despite the directness of his approach, Andy said it with love and care for her as a person, which came across in the way he spoke to her. He didn't have to try to act a certain way; he believed in her as a leader in his business and wanted her to drop this behaviour, so he needed to find out what was *really* going on.

The result was that she broke down and opened up to him about some challenges she was having in her personal life. He listened as she explained and empathised with her experience. Overnight, her behaviour changed.

Andy's approach is backed up in the fantastic book *Radical Candor* by former CEO coach at Dropbox and Twitter, Kim Scott.[22] In it, she shares a framework for giving feedback that combines two key traits of caring personally and challenging directly. Scott explains that we need both together to have meaningful feedback conversations which elicit behaviour change.

Leadership bias

A combination of directness and compassion is something that we can all practise. Unfortunately, many leaders have a habit of judging people in their team to be better or worse than others, which directly affects people's belief in themselves and their ability.

Megan Reitz, a fantastic academic, mindfulness teacher and coach from Ashridge Business School, talks about us as leaders needing to be aware of our 'little list of people': the ones we listen to and the ones we don't.[23] This kind of bias leads us to allow some team members to grow, as they feel our strong intention for them and faith in their ability, while others may shrink as they feel the opposite. They feel our doubt in their capacity.

I'm not saying that we should ignore all our instincts about people. Of course, there are situations where someone isn't right for a particular job, but more often than not, I see employees' ability shrivel primarily because of a manager's lack of faith in them.

I have experienced this personally. When a manager doubted my ability, it created a lot of stress and anxiety. The doubt I felt from them led me to over-strive for their attention, constantly trying to prove myself (a habit I tend to fall into) and get them to like me (another habit). I struggled to sleep for months and felt unstable at work.

I started having panic attacks while in this job, due not just to my manager, but also to a culture of favouritism and bullying. One minute, I was the apple of the CEO's eye; the next minute, I was being ignored. The shift in boundaries was destabilising and I could feel my mental health plummeting.

Just the way that manager looked at me caused me to feel incapable. I know now that this was their own history playing out – they felt threatened by me and keen to protect their own territory, so deep down, they didn't want me to succeed. At the time, all I was aware of was they had no good intention towards me and it meant that my performance dipped as I wasted energy on feelings of anxiety and a lack of safety. I'm not saying I was blameless; I struggled to adapt to their individualistic approach and their extreme logic heightened my emotions. I couldn't relate.

Luckily, I got out of that job one year in. I didn't even work my notice period; I just spoke to HR, submitted my letter of resignation, picked up my things and walked – something I thought I would never do. I had seen the way the bullying and sidelining intensified for those who were leaving – unsurprisingly, the company had a high staff turnover – so I knew it would be bad for my mental health to stay.

Conversely, I have experienced the opposite kind of leadership where I found myself moving mountains and achieving things that I didn't realise were possible. I put this down to my manager at the time having deep faith in me. They had clear intention for how they wanted me to grow and gave me the space and autonomy to make it happen. More on autonomy later.

As leaders, if we can give people a real chance – and by that, I mean we cultivate an intention which is about a pure faith in their potential – more often than not, we will see them fly. We can ask ourselves, 'How would things be if I had undeniable faith in this person's potential?' Try it on for size. Each time you ask yourself the question, you can drop more deeply into meaning it.

At first, this may seem forced, but if you really want to mean it and practise meaning it, you will see results. Your practice could be as simple as saying nice things about someone you tend to be more critical towards.

Instead, notice when they are doing good work or their good traits.

A lot of management experts talk about 'catching someone doing something right'. It's so easy for us as leaders to notice the negative because our brains are wired for survival, which means they are wired to watch out for risks and things going wrong. Therefore, we need to practise the opposite: the ability to notice what's working even if it feels like a person is only operating at 30%. What's good in that 30%? What makes you hopeful for this person?

Nancy Kline, a world-renowned author and facilitator around listening and human potential, goes as far as to say we need to compliment people five times more than we would criticise them.[24] I remember reading that and taking a significant mental back step, realising I didn't do this, particularly at home. I felt a sense of guilt, one that I was determined to channel into doing better.

CASE STUDY: PAYING COMPLIMENTS

EPISODE 2: THE CONSCIOUS LEADERS PODCAST

To illustrate how someone practises complimenting rather than criticising, let me call on my second podcast guest, June Cory. June talked about practising paying compliments to people in her team to show her strong intention for them. These compliments might be something about how they handled a particular phone call or a piece of client feedback; they could even be about their handbag (she's a particular fan of a Mulberry herself).

She reported that at first, this felt forced. Saying the compliments out loud seemed awkward, but in time, they just became a natural part of her conversation.

Is this a 'fake it until you make it' kind of thing? In a way, yes, it is. Giving both compliments and direct feedback (see previous case study) that cultivate faith in your employees and the individual habits that follow is about practice. It is translating intention into habit and making it real. Watch the results.

The principle here is one of trust. Some people say that others have to 'earn their trust' or 'trust can be easily broken', so what role do we have as leaders in that dynamic? Someone might break our trust because they don't feel comfortable enough to speak to us. If someone breaks our trust and we show how we still care about them, even though we're not happy with the behaviour, this is powerful. It separates our respect for the individual from our unhappiness with the particular task or behaviour. Our intention is still strong.

The power of intention

To apply this at a company or cultural level, let's talk about my client, Hable. Hable is a small business which has grown significantly and now exceeds thirty-eight internal employees. The leadership team recently hired a new COO as they are going through a process of professionalisation of what they do.

This is potentially a difficult process for employees as they have to adapt to change and implement a lot more systems and processes. Some of these measures are less popular than others. Luckily, Hable specialises in change management as a company. The leadership team recognises that they need to build awareness of why the change is happening and what the implications are, as well as being involved in the process. More significantly, they have a strong and clear intention around it.

Mark Reynolds, Hable's CEO, said to me, 'We are asking ourselves, "How do we grow while preserving our soul?"'[25] While this is a big question, it's also a practical one for us all to keep asking ourselves. It means that answers will drip-feed themselves into our psyche.

Andy Woodfield, who I introduced you to earlier in this chapter, believes that with a clear intention, we can say almost anything. If we're clear on what we believe about someone, even if the words don't come out in exactly the right order, the person will sense what we mean.

A well-prepared feedback meeting that lacks care for the individual will come across poorly. Don't fall into this trap. If you don't think you can offer this kind of intention, it's worth checking yourself and perhaps getting some one-to-one support to work through it. This is not a failure; by getting support from a nonjudgemental friend or a professional coach to overcome a barrier you may be facing with a particular individual, you can work through it.

Too often, we act in a way that seems to be the easy option, the quick win. When someone gets underneath our skin in a negative way, it is a big opportunity for learning on all sides.

Use it.

KEY TAKEAWAYS

- Strong and clear intention is about an attitude towards someone that's not clouded or jaded, but steeped in care and good ethics.

- The strength of your intention pays off in the most difficult moments – it allows directness.

- Continually ask yourself the question, 'How would it be if I had undeniable faith in this person's potential?'

- If you are struggling to offer positive feedback to a particular individual, get support.

PRACTICAL WAYS TO DEVELOP A CLEAR INTENTION

- Invite and act on feedback.

- Encourage a culture of appreciation, eg thank-you sessions.

- Focus on what's working. Cultivate a 5:1 ratio of positive to negative feedback.

- Tune in to someone's personal needs (as much as they want to share).

6
Lesson 2: Actively manage yourself

I'll start with a simple but significant example from a CEO called Nicole Sadd who I interviewed for the Conscious Leaders Podcast. She shared how she managed herself effectively during a tough period.

Nicole was in a high-pressure situation as she was a CEO in hospitality during the COVID-19 pandemic and lockdowns of 2020–2021. Daily, she was undergoing blow after blow of bad news. I had known her for a good few years before our interview and she always struck me as a resilient person: someone who had a lot of stamina for the tough times. At times during the pandemic, though, she noticed that she felt stressed and worn down by the sheer extreme and unpredictable nature of the situation.

In some moments, she had to hide herself away from group community calls. She knew that the calls were run well by another member of her leadership team, so she chose to stay away. Most of the time, she had strong visibility throughout the pandemic, but she knew her limits. The consistency in her behaviour was important so she could provide stability for others.

We can argue the merits or not of that choice, but what she recognised was the impact of her own behaviour on others. This kind of self-awareness is vital. It is the foundation of the strengths of a leader.

Another podcast guest, Charlotte Williams, a young leader of influencer marketing agency SevenSix, shared how she has learnt to recognise the early warning signs of her stress. She has a passion for beauty treatments and when she needs time out, she will treat herself, for example by getting her nails done. She also credits her nephew, a baby at the time of our interview, for his healing power. Charlotte has learnt that family and self-care are what she needs to nourish herself.

As a leader, you need to manage your own mood state. Otherwise, to a greater or lesser extent, you will infect others with your mood. This doesn't mean you can't be real and say when things are tough, but it does mean that your own emotional stability is important.

The neuroscience of mirroring behaviour

The value of managing our own reactivity is backed up by neuroscience. Clearly, the way we behave directly affects others, but this is significant even in subtle ways that relate to the wiring in our brains.

We have mirror neurons which allow us to learn through imitation. In other words, the behaviour of one person can create a mirror effect in the behaviour of another. This has dramatic positive effects when we think of children growing up and learning by imitation, and the learning of languages in context. It also sheds light on the merits of work-shadowing, such as a new recruit becoming familiar with the nuances of sales through relationship building. It is often much easier to watch an expert in action than it is to learn a skill in a theoretical context. We pick up cues in subtle ways.

These effects are deeper than we may think. The *Harvard Business Review* reported that 'when we consciously or unconsciously detect someone else's emotions through their actions, our mirror neurons reproduce those emotions'.[26] It follows on to say that 'these neurons create an instant sense of shared experience'. This shows the huge value of managing yourself and creating a positive mood among employees as it affects the emotions they will experience and their subsequent capacity.

I have also seen the effects of mirror neurons play out negatively. In my experience as an employee with one company, I watched toxic behaviour trickle down from the CEO to the senior management. This will have been due partly to conscious survival and self-preservation behaviours and partly entirely unconscious mirroring.

The CEO was a narcissist. They would blow hot and cold, exhibiting friendly behaviour at some times and point-blank ignoring employees at others. Theirs was a manipulative position, which meant that others frantically chased around for the praise they sought. The mood that the CEO walked in with radically affected everybody's day. Everyone was at the mercy of their mood state. When the rest of the leadership team began to behave like this too, the inconsistency and manipulation was toxic for employees.

This was an extreme situation, but people can detect even subtle inconsistencies in others' moods. We may not even have to say anything for others to be affected by our mood; they may just be able to feel it.

As humans, we are highly sensitive to the mood of others. This is why it is really important for us as leaders to create more stability in our emotional state.

CASE STUDY: EMOTIONAL STABILITY

To give you a good example of someone who focused on managing their mood, I worked with a client who was a leader in an organisation. Let's call her Janine.

Janine had some significant self-management and self-esteem issues. No one was aware of this, but it played out in the form of negativity and gossiping with certain members of the team rather than taking an objective approach. She would give narrow answers rather than looking at things from a broad perspective.

When she came to me, we worked on her solidity and reasons for bumping up against situations at work. At first, I found she just needed to be heard. She felt she was seen as draining at times in her organisation; someone who, despite all her ability, was bringing too much negativity. I heard her out.

What became clear to her as she talked was that she was putting too much focus and emotional energy into the negative. Part of the reason for this was her unhappiness in her own skin; she was demonstrating some of her low self-esteem.

To make that tangible, I helped her understand things like her own values, where they were being compromised and how she could assert the change she wanted to see within her area of control and influence. Without doing that, she couldn't rationalise why she was unhappy. This gave her a framework of solidity in the things she cared about and how she could communicate them more effectively.

We also worked on mindfulness. She undertook a six-week mindfulness for leaders course with me, which included daily practice.

Any good long-term practice needs focus and a sense of measure or balance about our experience, even if it is difficult in reality. I often ask people, 'Are you practising focus and calm or are you practising distraction and reactivity?' It's all too easy for us to practise the latter. Adrenaline is addictive, so it is tempting to be continually doing and winding ourselves up in our own thoughts (which are often playing on repeat when we are stressed).

Janine experienced this stress. Her daily mindfulness work involved practising being controlled, nonreactive and still. Over time, the wirings in the brain change with this kind of regular mindfulness practice. What this gave Janine was the perspective to step back and see a wider, more balanced view on situations.

For example, Janine's manager – one of the most senior in the company and based in the United States – was busy and stressed himself, so he did not pay her much attention. He would just bring her problems which did not fit into her strategy and expect her to sort them out without listening to her situation. He was too busy to have enough regard for her strategic plan.

After becoming practised in her daily mindfulness work, Janine was able to assert her competency more clearly with a positive energy. As a result, her manager started listening.

What's interesting is that her manager wasn't managing his own mood state effectively either. It was waterfalling down to her and she had to cope with this as well as her own issues. Hence, mindfulness work needs to start as near to the top in an organisation as possible, but even at the middle-management level, we can stop the mood proliferation in its tracks. Both Janine and her direct reports benefited (as did her manager who could learn a thing or two).

Janine and I worked together for six months, once a month. In that time, she moved a few internal mountains and emerged much more rational and focused. She stopped her over-dedication and long hours, which she realised were not actually productive in the long term.

I don't doubt that Janine is still experiencing challenges at work, but her own self-reflective work has enabled her to change her approach to dealing with them. She is now able to bring more perspective and become a productive member of the leadership team, rather than being at odds with them.

I have been on a journey of self-management and self-development (and still am). The issues that I have had with anxiety and low mood started when I was working in corporate business, managing big events that move around Europe (something I reflect on positively later).

I woke up one night in a cold sweat, having what I now know as a panic attack. From there, I started catastrophising and seeing the worst possible outcomes to lots of situations. The panic attacks continued. I felt isolated in my role and like the buck stopped with me.

The reality was, it didn't, and I did have support, but I had got myself into a position where I kept getting triggered into spirals of worry. These always popped up in the lead up to events I was running. I would expect them to magically disappear afterwards, but they wouldn't; they would stick around.

You may be aware of the fight or flight response. For those who aren't, it's the over-stimulation of the amygdala, the fight or flight centre in the brain, which causes us to release an excess of stress hormones such as adrenaline and cortisol. The amygdala can increase in size and activity through excess stress, which can cause a vicious circle. Even after the stressor has passed, we get stuck in stress mode.

For me, I felt like I was broken. I would frequently be found in the self-help section of a bookshop, looking for something to fix me. I would trawl the internet for articles on anxiety, only to find that at the end of reading them, I felt worse. The tips were too simplified, so I just fell deeper into my own unhappiness.

The thing with anxiety is that it often goes hand in hand with depression, or low mood as I like to call it. At times, I oscillated between anxious and down, finding it hard to get out of bed.

In the past, I've been a bit of a sceptic, so I wouldn't have considered myself a 'mindfulness type'. I lived in Oxford in 2011 when Oxford University was one of the leading institutions researching mindfulness. If it was good enough for Oxford, it was worth me taking a look.

At first, I did some self-study with the fantastic book *Mindfulness: Finding peace in a frantic world* by Mark Williams and Danny Penman.[27] Professor Mark Williams was the head of the Oxford University Centre for Mindfulness at the time and, with meditation teacher and journalist Danny Penman, he produced a book that is truly practical and accessible; I recommend it at least once a week.

From there, I took an eight-week MBCT training course, then I repeated it (as I was still knee-deep in anxiety the first time around). After that, without any particular plan, I took on mindfulness teacher training beside my corporate work.

The science of mindfulness

Mindfulness can reduce the size of the amygdala – that fight or flight centre – by half, meaning that the amygdala is able to return to normal conditions quickly after a stressful event. Mindfulness also increases the levels of grey matter in the hippocampus, which is the centre of decision making, self-control and self-regulation in the brain.[28] This is live evidence of neuroplasticity, the ability for the brain to evolve over time.

Ever called yourself undisciplined? It turns out, like many things, you can train in improving this. The problem is that people equate it to one-off or short-term meditation training. I'm talking about eight-week MBCT courses where people are practising mindfulness for thirty to fifty minutes daily, although evidence shows that people can see change from as little as ten minutes a day.[29] To put it simply, everyone is different, but in general, the more you put in, the more you get out.

Mindfulness had shown me that change is possible, but it is not a quick fix at all; it's a discipline, a practice. What became apparent when I first tried it was that I wasn't undergoing some kind of calm-inducing practice. It's a common misconception that mindfulness is about escaping from stress and obtaining a state of calm. Rather than escapism, mindfulness is tuning in. By tuning in, I was (and still am) developing a non-judgemental awareness of my moment-to-moment experience. This is a powerful mode that I hadn't been taught before.

To link this back to my own behaviour, I found I became less reactive, angry and anxious, and more considered. I gained a lot of familiarity with patterns and habits that we all share as humans, so I could make better choices about how to behave. For me, choice brings freedom. I'm not claiming that things have had a straight trajectory since; I have had setbacks, but I'm continuing this process for myself and have seen it bear fruits for me as well as for clients and friends who are on a similar path.

Some leaders hesitate to take on this work, asking themselves, 'Will I lose my edge?' They think that by practising mindfulness, they will somehow go all mushy. I have experienced the opposite: mindfulness, when it's taught properly, increases our focus, discipline, creativity and compassion as well as reducing stress. I teach leaders in a six-week mindfulness for leaders course and have seen their minds sharpen, their over-striving loosen and their stress reduce.

CASE STUDY: FROM ADRENALINE JUNKIE TO REGULAR MEDIATOR

EPISODE 1: THE CONSCIOUS LEADERS PODCAST

My first guest on the podcast, John Hesler, runs four construction companies and an investment company. He shared his change in behaviour and approach to self-management.

In his early years in business, by his own admission, he was a go-getter – a brash, pushy man, ready to squeeze suppliers and wield his own power. John was brought up with the understanding that if a bully picked on him, he should find a brick and throw it at them. They would then know not to mess with him again. He was also an adrenaline junkie and spent lots of time doing extreme sports. All of this finally caught up with him when he blacked out on a sky dive. He was a millionaire, but had suffered adrenal burnout getting there.

Through therapy and a lot of family support, John recovered over two years. After our first meeting, he also took up meditation. He now meditates for twenty minutes twice a day as a strict habit.

In a conversation after our podcast interview, I explored more deeply what a meditation practice brings him. He reported that meditation allows him to tune into others much more easily; it brings him an empathy and awareness of their habits and patterns. Beyond other people, it allows him to understand his own habits and patterns and helps him change his behaviour in an instant.

For example, John said that he was talking to his dad and started shouting and arguing with him. He hadn't shouted for years and noticed he was reverting to past behaviour, so he stopped in his tracks, stood back and calmed down.

He reported that in the past, as a leader, he would be much more wound up by his employees and certain people would really trigger him. Now he says he can look at people with more of an open-heart.

He said, 'No one is actively trying to piss me off. Everyone is just trying to find their own way and [they] come with their own issues.'[30] This shift in thinking is possible due to his ongoing meditation, which helps him stay calm and reason with people.

KEY TAKEAWAYS

- Manage your own mood state, otherwise you risk infecting others with your mood.

- The transmission of mood is down to mirror neurons, which means people naturally reflect the behaviour of others.

- An evidence-based mindfulness practice is a way of rewiring your brain to support you in your self-management endeavours.

PRACTICAL WAYS TO ACTIVELY MANAGE YOURSELF

- Find ways that work for you and support your wellbeing, eg meditation, exercise, time in nature, time for mind-wandering, time out with friends etc.

- Create habits and implement them regularly in your life.

7
Lesson 3: Deepen your listening skills

Listening is one of our most undervalued skills. We know when we are not being listened to. We might leave a conversation feeling unsure, downtrodden or slightly empty. We might have had a lot of advice come our way, but we have a sense that the other person hasn't understood our situation.

In this chapter, I will share some of my own experience and bring in examples from leaders who show great listening skills. Some demonstrate a culture of listening which has huge benefits you may not even realise are possible.

In his book *The 7 Habits Of Highly Effective People*, Stephen Covey says, 'Most people do not listen with the intent to understand; they listen with the intent to reply.'[31] I remember reading these words many years ago and it hit me – was I listening to understand or simply to reply with my thoughts? To be completely honest with you, it was the latter.

Historically, I was not good at listening. I looked back at some comments from when I was about eighteen – apparently, I was the one always trying to convince people to think something different. Fantastic. There was some jumped-up young person ready to tell others that they were wrong. I realised I was often trying to convince people to change their mind rather than understanding their perspective. It wasn't until I trained properly in mindfulness for myself that I realised what I had been missing out on.

There are many barriers to listening – we will all have our own.

For me, they were things like distraction, impatience and control. If we really listen, we need to be patient and repeatedly bring our attention back to the other person. If I was in a mode of not listening effectively, the first few seconds of a conversation could be difficult. My impatience would rise as the other person slowly got out their words.

I needed to cultivate patience so that I could drop into a listening mode and settle into the process. In this chapter, I will talk more about how leaders can effectively do this and discuss podcast examples that show where it really works.

Deep listening requires a sense of letting go rather than controlling. If we're constantly chipping in with our thoughts and opinions, we're controlling. We're fuelling our need for adrenaline and doing. What we sacrifice consequently is the headspace of the other person.

A lot of the time, we experience a lack of good listening in normal conversation. We chime in, commenting and sharing our own experience. Of course, this can be fun; it's sharp, back and forth. However, there are many disadvantages.

It doesn't allow space in a conversation for the people we're with to get to their real point. Instead, we start solving a problem at a superficial level before we've realised what the problem is *really* about. Their thinking has been limited.

Renowned author, speaker, and founder and president of Time to Think, Nancy Kline, says, 'The quality of your attention determines the quality of other people's thinking.'[32] We have the power to enable someone to think more clearly.

Most everyday conversation doesn't lend itself to different personality types. A lot of the time, people need some space to think and really be heard. If there isn't that space, they will stay quiet and others will think they have nothing to add. What is key in listening skills is how you *are* for the other person; what you say is less important. This skill is much more in the being than it is in the doing.

Let me illustrate by sharing four practices that I identify in great listening, alongside the podcast guests who shared these skills. Anyone can improve any of these.

1: Grounding/presence

A person who is a good listener is grounded, but the reality is, many of us are not grounded much of the time. We spend our time darting between virtual or physical meetings, and we may arrive in body, but not in mind. Simple grounding practices can help us arrive more fully.

Personally, I have been practising mindfulness for twelve years, so a morning meditation plus small meditations throughout the day help me reground. Everyone is different, so acknowledging whatever helps you ground is important. It could be walking, music or writing a few notes. Even if it's something small to take the edge off a frazzled mind, it's useful.

I'll delve a little more into the meditation practice so you can understand some of what I have learnt over the last few years. The key for me is not to expect myself to become grounded, but to ground myself *in* whatever I am experiencing. This means there is no goal other than to tune into my state of mind and body and feel the earth.

Many people are under the illusion that they need to get good at meditation – somehow more and more zen. They say to me they have tried meditation and don't like it because they are not good at it. What they mean is that it is uncomfortable, so they give up.

Mindfulness is the opposite. It is pausing and acknowledging whatever is there at that time. In practice, mindfulness is about continually returning to a point of focus and repeatedly putting down the habits of the mind that take us elsewhere.

I often say that meditation is 'tuning in, not zoning out'. For many, this is not easy at first, so I encourage you to stay with it and practise. By sticking with it, you are training your mind to be present with what is. The Buddhists say that most of us spend our lives in 'craving' and 'aversion', ie longing for some things and pushing away others.[33] Meditation is the opportunity to practise the here and now. To be with yourself as you are.

In terms of how presence links to listening, I experienced this in a dramatic way on a silent mindfulness retreat. These retreats have become a regular part of my personal growth where I spend a week together with perhaps fifty to sixty people. The teachers speak when they are teaching or guiding meditation, but we as participants remain in silence.

My first retreat took place over three days and three nights. What struck me about one of the teachers was his deep sense of groundedness and presence. Even the way he first walked in the room; I remember the energy changing. I felt more relaxed in my body and became more focused. In a roomful of sixty people, it would be easy to feel distracted, yet we weren't; our attention heightened in that moment.

I experienced this even more in small groups where we had a short chance to share and speak with the teacher as part of the retreat. He would listen deeply to us. I would find these moments of being witnessed by others moving and emotional; there was no busy-ness in their reply to mask over my emotions. I was just sitting there with five other people who listened to me. The teacher's presence was evident and we were all clearly moved by it.

This is an extreme example of a highly trained mindfulness teacher who has been doing this stuff for about thirty years, so I don't want to set the bar too high here. The key point this example illus-trates is that by being present and listening to us, he made sure we felt really heard. In those twenty minutes together, we all processed something, yet little was said by him. He would reflect back a few things and perhaps offer us some pointers, but in general, he was creating a space for us to express ourselves.

When I experienced the power of someone's presence this profoundly, it hit me how much I had been missing out on, both in being listened to and in offering a listening space to others.

2: Strong intention

As we learnt in the previous chapter, bringing a clear, strong intention to your listening is vital. You might want to hold the person in mind before you speak to them and think about your intention for them. It's important they know you care.

This is about putting your employees as the experts at the centre of your focus. It may be that in the past, your leadership style has been more directive, so what would it be like to defer to them to help them practise being the ones with solutions and answers? I have heard various techniques for doing this, but none will work if you don't genuinely believe that employees have the answers. Hone your positive intention and practise acting it out, over and over.

I love the way my podcast guest June Cory said that leadership is about 'picking people up who aren't doing well and helping them to do better, getting the people that are doing OK to do better still and getting high achievers to absolutely soar'.[34] This shows her strong intention for employees, regardless of where their performance is at that time.

3: Curiosity

This is about bringing a genuine interest in what a person is saying alongside a lack of judgement or even knowledge of what they are about to say. The Buddhists call this a 'don't know mind'. What this does is allow the person to express themselves without feeling judged.

We can communicate this simply by the look on our faces, showing interest and curiosity. If we ask a question and genuinely want the other person to answer it, that's dramatically different to giving them the impression that we know what we expect the answer to be. If we show openness to anything, shut up and ask good questions, who knows what deep knowledge and ideas we might get from our teams?

Podcast guest Jean Baptiste Oldenhove, a leader in the sustainability and investment world, is a big fan of curiosity. It is a mode he's always wanting to uphold. His company brings together multiple international public and private stakeholders to make large investments in sustainability projects. For that to be successful, he needs to be curious to understand what motivates people and their language style so he can tune into them. This deep sense of curiosity leads to understanding, which in turn allows people to feel heard.

If people feel heard, they feel connected and that their relationship is building with you. Commonly, people don't feel heard, so when you step up and become really curious, this is powerful.

Many people think listening is something they *should* be good at, so the idea of training in it sounds strange. In reality, it is something that we all need to practise regularly. At first, when we practise, it may not feel that we are good at it. This is because we are moving a skill from the unconscious to the conscious.

It's useful for us to look to the Conscious Competence Ladder, developed by Noel Burch at Gordon Training International in the 1970s.[35] This states that there are four levels of learning:

- Unconscious incompetence

- Conscious incompetence

- Conscious competence

- Unconscious competence.

When I train leaders in listening, they initially move from unconscious incompetence to conscious incompetence. In other words, they move into the unknown in a skill they feel they should be good at, but competence takes practice. This can be humbling but it gets better quickly.

One of the leaders I spoke to who demonstrates curiosity really well is Ciaron Dunne, CEO of Genie Ventures, a medium-sized company based in Cambridge with employees UK-wide. He has an enquiring mind and the people around him see his openness.

Ciaron realises the power of bringing energy to conversations through interest and adding dynamism. That energy, he finds, allows employees to open up and express themselves more fully. As a historically shy person, he finds this is a conscious act that he is not naturally good at. He intentionally brings curiosity to conversations to help engage other people and reports that this results in much more motivation among employees.

4: Empathy

Empathy is a key leadership quality. It's subtly but significantly different to sympathy; empathy is putting yourself in someone else's shoes and knowing or imagining what that must feel like. Indeed, the American Psychological Association's *Dictionary of Psychology* describes it as 'understanding a person from his or her frame of reference rather than one's own, or vicariously experiencing that person's feelings, perceptions, and thoughts'.[36]

Sympathy is just feeling sorry for someone and is pretty useless. It can easily have a negative impact as pity may not go down well nor help the person to feel better. Best avoided.

Daniel Goleman has recognised three types of empathy.[37] Cognitive empathy is the ability to understand another person's perspective; emotional empathy is the ability to feel what someone else feels; and empathic concern is the ability to sense what another person needs from you. Clearly, this links not only to our neurobiological needs to be understood and cared for, but also to our ability to act in a way that is supportive.

This often isn't what we see in organisations. Even in organisations where there is broad agreement that empathy is a fundamental skill that people need to be showing, there tends to be an absence of it. Indeed, there are big gaps between how leaders and employees see empathy in an organisation, with CEOs typically perceiving there to be much higher levels present than employees experience.[38]

Empathy allows you to touch into the emotion of another person to care and support them. A lot of leaders complain that they feel like their employees' therapist or babysitter. You don't have to be a therapist or a babysitter, but you do need to be there for their personal needs in some form. Often, leaders are overstretched or don't look after their own wellbeing, which means they have less capacity to support others. They lack emotional availability. This is costly because personal issues will get in the way of someone's wellbeing and productivity.

Emotional availability doesn't mean that everyone wants to open up; of course, it's down to the individual how much they trust you or feel comfortable sharing. Sometimes, you don't need to hear a lot of detail to be there for them and know that there is a lot going on in their personal life. As a leader, you can show empathy as simply as offering them more space, time or whatever else they need to feel supported.

This is where sharing something about yourself can be useful. You will know if you are in a situation with an employee who would benefit from hearing your story, especially if there are parallels with theirs. These moments of vulnerability, be they with an individual or a group, are powerful. In sharing something about yourself, you open up the ability to connect with people. More on vulnerability later.

All of these aspects of listening allow us to get beyond the superficial and find out what a conversation is *really* about, so we can show understanding and take practical action where necessary. Often, when someone argues with a colleague, it is not about the colleague at all; it is about a struggle the individual is undergoing personally which makes them more reactive. If we are able to support them in some way, we can help them get to the root of the problem so they can recognise it and solve it at its source.

Sometimes, a simple question at the end of a conversation such as 'Anything else you need to say?' or 'Anything you are worried about that it would help to share?' allows the other person to tell you more about what is going on, as long as you stay present and really listen. This is sometimes where the *real* reason they are angry / upset comes out. It is easy to talk on a superficial level, but if you show you genuinely want to know about the other person and help them, that changes things.

From my experience, this work takes practice and experimentation to see what level of depth is right for each employee. Some employees will feel comfortable opening up and others less so, so it's right that you follow their lead. This will allow all employees to build trust in you over time. This can also be a cultural thing, where a culture of openness, listening, empathy etc spreads throughout a group.

 CASE STUDY: TRANSFORMING ENGAGEMENT
EPISODE 25: THE CONSCIOUS LEADERS PODCAST

My podcast guest Lee Timbrell is a clear leader in employee engagement. Lee is a general manager at

Vision Labs, owned by Specsavers, and runs three
manufacturing and distribution sites of around
750 people.

When he was new to his first posting, the company
discovered that employee engagement was really low.
Indeed, it carried out regular surveys to gauge morale,
among other measures, and it had hit an all-time low of
6.9/10. The leadership team set about having meetings
with all of the staff in groups of about thirty. They
were open about the poor results from the survey and
wanted to hear what was going so terribly wrong.

Lee reported that the meetings were brutal as
employees fed information upwards to leaders who had
previously been out of touch with what was going on.
They listened. Indeed, they didn't just listen once; they
took on board what employees said across the different
groups, and then reported back and listened more. The
result was that engagement skyrocketed to a fantastic
9.1/10.

Lee was then asked to do the same thing at the
company's Southampton site, where he would take
on the leadership role to improve engagement. Again,
the leaders listened and their humility around what
the employees had said, along with their willingness to
make change, had a massive impact on staff morale.

CASE STUDY: LISTENING WITH INTEREST

Another person who has taught me a lot about listening
is my friend and therapist, Nick Heap. Nick is one of the
wisest people I know and he embodies great listening
better than anyone else I've come across. His eyes show

empathy and compassion, and he's comfortable sitting in warm silence while I get whatever is going on in my life off my chest.

When I quizzed him about his inspiration for such great listening, he talked about one of his first bosses at a scientific organisation when he was a research chemist. He reported that his boss would come in every day, put his foot on a stool and ask simple open questions like 'What happened yesterday?' or 'What have you found out?' Nick said that his boss's deep sense of interest was so motivating, his listening so gentle and encouraging, that Nick worked twelve-hour days because he wanted to have stimulating things to say to him.

At another organisation's team day, Nick had a revelation about how people could work effectively. He said, 'We could solve all the problems in this organisation if we just listened to each other.' A senior leader heard this and said it wasn't just the solution to their issues, but was also the solution to the questions over the world's biggest problems. At this point, Nick realised listening would be his life's work.

Nick took steps to work in the field of listening. He became a Samaritan, and then went on to work for the Marriage Guidance Council (later RELATE) where he received some magnificent training. He said this journey is all about self-awareness; it's hard to listen to someone else if you don't know who you are, so behind good listening is a lot of self-discovery.

Practically, Nick told me, listening is the foundational social skill. Every time we are listened to properly (ie we know and feel that the other person is listening), it 'tunes up our mind' and helps us think. Our emotions can become blocked, but when we listen, we can help people express their emotions. They might laugh or cry or express themselves in another way, but it all helps them release those emotions.

Nick said the main benefits to great listening for leaders are: the motivation that comes from it; the opportunity to know what's really going on; the great ideas that emerge; and the increase in clarity of mind for the employee.

Listening and being present

Personally, I took my listening a long way when training as a coach. This was quite an emotional time for me. I covered an intense amount of co-coaching with other trainees and that meant we all went through our own journey.

The power of having that intensity of listening and support meant that I could process a lot. At the time, my business was young, which meant making things add up financially was a struggle. I still had some hang-ups from my previous employer and childhood, and I had a deep desire to prove myself. This proving, striving and pushing meant I was putting a lot of pressure on myself both in my business and socially.

Spending time being listened to deeply really supported me to settle into myself, which is something I still work on. The crying that resulted was cathartic.

The only reason I wouldn't cry in front of others in the past was the fear of how the other person would feel. Having learnt a lot about the release that comes from crying, I'm now keen to embrace it.

Often, if you observe someone when they cry, there is a surge of emotion, which allows them space afterwards to process their feelings. World-renowned listening expert, Nancy Kline, says that crying allows emotional release to restore thinking.[39] Therefore, allowing someone to cry, without stopping them, is a good thing – they are processing their emotions and are usually able to think more clearly afterwards.

All the techniques and models I learnt during my coaching training are interesting, but they have no value if I don't first work on how I show up for the other person, how I can be present. By cultivating our presence, we readily think of how to support someone more skilfully in the moment. This is as opposed to using a premeditated solution or continually thinking about what to do next. If we're thinking of techniques and ideas when communicating with someone, we can't be listening fully.

We need to stay present with our clients, employees, friends and relatives – grounded, curious, empathetic with strong intention – as well as we can. This takes work.

When you start practising listening, not only are you likely to feel somewhat incapable, you'll also feel tired. This is normal. It may feel like you are not doing much, but this is about showing up in a way that is conducive to the other person thinking more clearly. You are cultivating presence. This all takes effort, but the more you practise, the more it will become natural and easy over time.

The emotional energy that goes into listening deeply is tiring, but it has the potential to be charging and extremely powerful at the same time, especially when we see results. Many people go into leadership thinking it's about making all the good decisions and controlling things, but most conscious and success-ful leaders barely make any decisions. What they are doing is making themselves emotionally available to their leadership teams and employees, while remain-ing aware that they need the right systems around them so they can recharge.

KEY TAKEAWAYS

- Distraction, impatience and control are barriers to us in listening.

- Listening can involve falling on your sword – be prepared for it to be a humbling process.

- Great listening is a practice – one that takes energy. Resource yourself for it and be patient with your progress as you hone your skills.

PRACTICAL WAYS TO DEEPEN YOUR LISTENING SKILLS

Set yourself up for great listening by using these four key elements:

1. Grounding

2. Strong intention

3. Curiosity

4. Empathy

8
Lesson 4: Lean into difficult situations

It is apt that this chapter follows on from Lesson 3 on listening as the foundations for dealing with difficulty certainly lie here. Let's explore first what we mean by difficult. This is anything that feels like it is uncomfortable. It could be poor behaviour that means we need to give some feedback. It could be a fall out between employees or within a team.

It's not good to start from a point of blame. People are rarely point-blank idiots just for the sake of it. There will be a story behind their behaviour, which means the person may be experiencing difficulties at home; they may feel underconfident or isolated at work; they may be in the wrong job and find that their role isn't playing to their strengths.

In terms of having difficult conversations, we will all have different attitudes to this. Some of us will feel confident, others will feel fearful. While I now quite enjoy these moments of honesty, it hasn't always been the case.

Let's revisit Anne, the difficult coaching client I mentioned near the beginning of the book. I used to get myself quite worked up about my sessions with her. Most of the fear I felt was around my own inadequacy in handling the situation; yes, she was a difficult case, but I toggled between confidence that I could do it and help her overcome her challenges, and having a lack of belief in myself.

She would have felt that imbalance within me, which showed my newness as a coach. I still felt like I needed her approval or her to like me. Yes, this is a natural human response, but I had to work more on my own stability within myself so that I no longer craved her approval. I was her coach, not her friend.

I recognised my own progress recently when dealing with another coaching client. Admittedly, he is a much easier client than Anne, but we came across something he wasn't comfortable with. I felt confident sitting in that discomfort with him and helping him work through his answers. He would have felt my confidence.

> When we feel uncomfortable, it is reassuring to feel the steadfastness of someone else.

Many leaders and managers are worried about their employees and their issues. This feeling of worry will be felt by the employees.

Effective ways to address difficult situations

Back to Lee Timbrell from Specsavers. I named his podcast episode 'Being a rock for others' because his stability and strength came across as he described how he navigated difficult situations with employees. He commented that being direct with people rather than 'flowery and fluffy' was critical to his success with them. He cared; he meant it, so he shared with them to help them grow.

Awareness is the first step to conquering fear. From a point of awareness, you are able to seek the change you want. Good questions to ask yourself are 'What would I do if I weren't afraid?'; 'What would I say if I weren't afraid?'; 'How could I be for this person to support their growth?' I invite you to hold these gently as open questions; do not search frantically for answers, but wait for the answers to emerge.

Annette Jensen, who is a great friend of mine in organisational development, said:

'Many leaders are afraid or don't know how to give good feedback. Their inability to create trust often stems from their inability to have difficult conversations. I feel trust is at the core of the best relationships, at home or work.'[40]

People often fear that difficult conversations will erode positive relationships, but Annette emphasises how they actually build the trust you need.

Andy Woodfield, the partner at PwC we met in Chapter 5, is a master at giving direct feedback. In fact, one of the most impressive stories he told me was about giving feedback to a client. In this situation, a senior person on the client side was not behaving in a way that was acceptable to him. They were using bullying behaviour, so Andy realised he needed to put a stop to it.

He spoke to them directly and said, 'If you want the best from my team, then this is not the way.'[41] It's easy to read these words in a flat way, but Andy was bringing his self-awareness, strong intention and ability to listen – all qualities we looked at in the previous chapters. He would have shown that he cared about the client as a human being too, alongside his staff.

The result was that the client opened up about some challenges that they had going on in their life. As a result, their behaviour changed overnight. When his team asked what had happened and how he had managed to achieve that, Andy's response was that this client was going through some difficult times, but had acknowledged their behaviour. The client had opened up to him in confidence and he was going to keep it that way; all his team needed to know was that there were deeper reasons behind the poor behaviour that had been playing out.

Poor behaviour always comes from somewhere, so we need to raise our awareness about its root cause. Great leaders like Andy, who are brave enough to face up to poor behaviour quickly and directly, aid this process. Most importantly, Andy was able to bring the cleanness of his intention to this potentially difficult conversation with his client. His faith and belief in the other person shone through so he could deliver a strong message that enabled them to open up.

Another of my podcast guests, Nicole Sadd, had the tough job of working as a CEO in hospitality through the COVID-19 pandemic. She did a lot of effective preventative work by leaning into small discomforts as soon as they arose. Regular check-ins with her team gave them all the opportunity to hear short personal stories from each other on a Monday. Often, people would be really open. She encouraged people to honour where they were at (my words, not hers) and would regularly talk with them as they came to her office, getting a sense if they weren't doing well and inviting them to share.

What she showed here was willingness, openness and compassion. She prioritises this as she knows that supporting people's welfare helps both them as individuals and the business.

Another guest who demonstrates a more overarching policy is Pip Jamieson, CEO of The Dots. She said that she has a zero tolerance policy on gossip. This means that if someone comes to her about someone else's behaviour, she asks them to speak to the person directly. She has also made this policy clear to all employees.

Every company would do well to adopt this policy. Gossip, however mild, is never helpful and quickly escalates into bigger issues. Too often, senior people get involved in it too, which is terrible role modelling. Pip catches these issues early and encourages others to lean into discomfort with each other.

Cheryl Luzet, the CEO of Wagada, opened up about her journey with being candid. Wagada is a digital marketing agency that hires lots of young people, so the leadership team needs to do some hands-on coaching to help them learn on the job. She revealed that previously with some colleagues, she didn't feel like she was honest enough because she was nervous about their anxieties or what they would think. She describes herself as an honest person and is now much more comfortable having direct conversations early on.

Wagada takes a light approach to failure. The leadership team wants to encourage people to talk about failure so everybody can learn from it. They even go so far as to pop the 'failure prosecco' if the business experiences a big failure so everyone can have a glass and talk about what went wrong and what they have learnt.

This is a fantastic idea. It opens up the dialogue and culture around failure so that people feel comfortable sharing the lows as well as the highs. Again, that awareness means they can change. Cheryl actively looks for an attitude of learning and humility in her new hires. She doesn't want know-it-alls; she wants people who are honest about *not* knowing the answers, but curious to go find them and learn from their mistakes.

'Discomfort' and 'difficulty' are rather negative words and I wish I didn't have to use them to make it clear what I am talking about. Sometimes, we can badge things as difficult so we slip into passive ways, avoiding the real issue. With some small but significant behaviour change, we have the chance to build more trust.

Research professor Brené Brown said, 'Clear is kind. Unclear is unkind.'[42] Feedback for someone is as much a gift for them as anything, as it involves you getting out of your comfort zone to allow them to grow. The alternative, as the quote shows so eloquently, is to stagnate their growth. Unkind indeed.

Here is a set of guidelines in dealing with the 'difficult', along with examples so you can see what I have learnt from the leaders I have interviewed on this subject, plus my own experience:

1. **Catch discomfort/drama early.** This can be done through regular check-ins with people in your immediate team or by going round and doing a live 'weather check' with the group to see how everyone is doing. You can get people to report the 'weather pattern' inside them, eg stormy, cloudy, blue skies, without the need to say anything further about it. You will soon know if someone's mood is low for a continual period and can check in more fully on a one-to-one basis. I appreciate that this can feel time-consuming, particularly when you have a lot of other things to do, but these conversations with people will show them that you care and help you catch a worry early before it spirals.

2. **Address it directly (with compassion).** There is nothing worse than feeling someone is avoiding discussing a topic with you, so if you have direct feedback for someone, give it to them straight.

The way to balance this so it doesn't come across as aggressive is to show care and compassion for the individual. This is back to your intention and how you feel about them. Andy Woodfield (who is a master at this) talked to his senior manager directly about her being super nasty. He couldn't have been more direct, but he also said that he knew her well enough to recognise this wasn't how she normally behaved and wonder what was going on for her. She felt his compassion.

3. **Listen deeply.** Use the methods I share – strong intention (so the other person feels your care), groundedness (so it doesn't feel like you're somewhere else), curiosity (so you're open to whatever they have to say) and empathy (so they feel understood) – or whatever works for you. When someone has just received direct feedback from you, it's your turn to hear from them. Bring your whole self to it as well as you can.

4. **Ask how you can support people to make change.** This step is powerful because it shows your openness – perhaps you are the problem here. It may be that you haven't explained something properly or they feel underconfident because of your behaviour. Asking how you can support and change shows a sense of humility and openness that is important for employees to see. It also shows that you are open to *their* feedback and is fantastic role modelling.

5. **Is there anything else?** This powerful question comes up again and again and will help you gain deeper insights. There may or may not be something else the other person wants to share, but if you ask with genuine curiosity, holding the silence afterwards for longer than you ordinarily would, then they may share more.

6. **Check in periodically.** If someone does open up to you, don't disappear afterwards. It may be that you need to give them a short call in a week's time to check on their progress.

KEY TAKEAWAYS

- Barriers to dealing with difficulties usually lie in our own busyness and fear of discomfort.

- We can work on our stability within ourselves to handle these situations skilfully and save time in the long run.

PRACTICAL WAYS TO LEAN INTO DIFFICULT SITUATIONS

- Six steps for dealing with the difficult:

  1. Catch discomfort or drama early.

  2. Address it directly.

  3. Listen deeply.

  4. Ask how you can support others to make change.

  5. Ask, 'Is there anything else?'

  6. Check in periodically.

- A zero tolerance policy on gossip is an effective strategy for preventing unnecessary drama at work.

9
Lesson 5: Give away power

Before we start on this chapter, I want to acknowledge how comfortable it is being in control. By control, I mean the need many leaders feel to manage things in detail, hold the majority of the knowledge about what is going on and maintain a high level of decision making.

Control feels good; it feels predictable. It may not be easy because it means that we are doing a lot. It means we have fingers in all the pies and – at risk of mixing too many metaphors – are juggling all of the balls.

In many ways, we have been conditioned for control. Most of our education systems were built around controllable outcomes such as exams and don't reward creativity and expression to the extent they should.

For the most part, no one teaches us how to give away power. Most of us as leaders find ourselves in a position of responsibility through either our passion or moving up the ranks. It feels the exception rather than the rule when we get the space to grow the attributes needed for a modern leader.

There are a few issues with control, the first being that it is not sustainable.

For us to grow and scale our initiatives in sustainable ways, we need to let them go so that others can take them forward. In turn, this allows people to grow.

 CASE STUDY: MASTERING AUTONOMY

EPISODE 16: THE CONSCIOUS LEADERS PODCAST

A podcast guest who shows a real understanding of how leaders can create more autonomy is Phil Wild. Phil is CEO at James Cropper, a brand you probably haven't heard of, but you may well have used its products. James Cropper produces speciality plastic-free packaging and advanced materials for other manufacturers and consumer brands.

Phil's take on autonomy is that we want to be asking people, 'How far out do we need to be thinking?' He goes on to say, 'As a leader, by forcing the topic of looking further and further out... you're going to be drawing yourself and others with you out of the more directional and tactical discussions, which allows you to delegate... Some find this easier than others.'[43]

He recognises that James Cropper is still on its own journey as a business with this. From my experience, most are. Sometimes as leaders, when we come into businesses, we are firefighting, but once things have settled a bit, Phil says that's when 'the horizon moves out'. He asks of his leadership team that they have a clear view of what things will look like in five years' time, then everything becomes stepping stones to support that.

CASE STUDY: SMALL BUSINESSES WITHIN A BUSINESS
EPISODE 7: THE CONSCIOUS LEADERS PODCAST

Ciaron Dunne, the CEO of Genie Ventures, talks about how he puts his company growth down to autonomy. His leadership team made some big shifts in the eighty-person organisation: they did away with centralised coding, marketing functions etc and decided that each part of the business would be more successful with its own mini-team. Each department became a small business which operates a high degree of autonomous decision making.

Ciaron sees the drawbacks of corporates that lack pace because work must go through so many different departments. If something lands with the IT, marketing etc team, it's not top of their list – they didn't necessarily decide to do it, which slows everything down.

He admits that there are sacrifices to be made with smaller, more autonomous structures within his business. For example, developers in separate teams won't benefit as much from each other's expertise. For Ciaron, the main benefit is pace.

'You can move much faster with small agile teams,' he says.[44] This is particularly well suited when you want to grow something quickly. He also reports that anecdotally, he sees it as a lot more rewarding for employees. There are high degrees of engagement shown by much enthusiasm for in-depth problem-solving situations that offer people agency to get stuck in and discover answers themselves.

At Genie Ventures, teams effectively operate as small businesses within a medium-sized business. They have all the benefits of small agile teams with the parallel security of the company's larger size. Ingenious! (Sorry, couldn't help myself.)

What autonomy leans towards is monitoring output as opposed to controlling input. Andy Woodfield says that we need to measure the outputs as opposed to focusing on what we put in.

Another drawback to control is that it doesn't allow for others to take true ownership of their work. Calling back on the work of Dan Pink, whose book *Drive: The surprising truth about what motivates us* talks about autonomy in some detail (alongside mastery and purpose as the three key drivers for human motivation),[45] ownership of our work allows us to grow and feel the reward of our outcomes. It is one of the key ways to help us thrive as people. For me, there is no greater work as a leader than to help people thrive.

CASE STUDY: UPSIDE DOWN MANAGEMENT

EPISODE 27: THE CONSCIOUS LEADERS PODCAST

A podcast guest that I absolutely adored meeting is Sir John Timpson CBE of high-street brand Timpson. Timpson is well known for key cutting and shoe repairs and at the time of writing has 2,000 stores and £20 million annual profit. John is now Chairman of Timpson, having passed the CEO role on to his son James twenty years ago.

John credits Timpson's success to its rigorous pursuit of the culture he calls 'upside down management'. It's a culture based on trust and kindness. He goes as far as to say, 'You don't tell people how to do the job; you're there [in head office] to make life easy... To help employees give the best service, especially those who are the most difficult, the only way... is to trust the people meeting your customers to do it the way they want.'[46]

In a practical sense, this means that the area managers are purely there to support those running the stores. John calls them Timpson's 'social workers' because they are not there to tell anyone what to do, but to support each employee as a whole person. As a result, area managers have the capacity to support in a way that helps themselves too. John has noticed that this plays out in wonderful ways, with one area manager helping a staff member move house on a weekend. Employees can also call on extra support such as loans from the company to help with financial hardship.

For me, what makes this most profound is the impact it has on the 10% of Timpson's staff who are ex-convicts. Timpson actively hires people coming out of prison to give them an opportunity. John says that one of the first jobs team leaders give these new recruits is something that shows they are trusted, such as taking money to the bank. This never fails.

This trust must be powerful if you are coming out of prison and most employers won't readily offer you that same opportunity. Suddenly, you have an employer on your side, ready to help you rebuild your life.

Letting go of power

John Hesler, my first podcast guest who suffered adrenal burnout from overdoing adventure sports as well as striving and pushing too hard in his business life, experienced huge change from giving away power. While spending a couple of years recovering from his burnout, he was forced to give up responsibility. Indeed, he said the severity of his burnout meant that had no energy to work. He wasn't in a fit state to lead his businesses, so the leaders he had employed had to step up.

He said to them, 'You need to decide this stuff for yourselves. If you fail, you fail, but I can't do it, so you just need to do your best.'[47]

As a by-product of his adrenal burnout, he discovered the transformational power of fully trusting others and letting go. From there, something incredible happened: he saw his businesses blossom much further and faster than he could have ever imagined. It makes me think of Eric Michael Leventhal's quote, 'We are at our most powerful the moment we no longer need to be powerful.'[48] In John letting go, his people were able to be empowered.

In the past, John thought that people said what he wanted to hear as he was someone who shouted and was intimidating at times. That led people to publicly agree with him even when they disagreed. John pointed to the example from *Alice's Adventures in Wonderland* where everyone around the Queen of Hearts is wearing fake big noses, ears and bellies to make her feel better about herself. The Queen gets to hear what she wants to hear.

When you hold all the control, people may lie to you as a leader to keep you happy, but when John experienced his burnout, his teams didn't have to keep him happy. They had to work as a collective.

When John gave away all that power, his businesses soared commercially and profitability went through the roof. He found his people were happier. Since then, he has never looked back. This is how he operates, not only for other people's success, but for his own space. He had been working twelve- to fourteen-hour days, seven days a week, and 75% of what he did was a waste of his time. Now he concentrates on the 25% that is actually worthwhile. Controlling people was hugely time-consuming and now he feels free.

Autonomy creates a real time-saving opportunity if it is supported by a culture of trust. I interviewed Steve O'Brien, CEO at Newicon, a software-development company, and he showed how trust can be built by small measures or even lack of measures.[49]

When the company started to grow, the leadership team asked the question, 'What's the expense policy?' Steve thought about it and wondered why they needed an expense policy at all. They all saw each other every day and trusted each other.

Not all his colleagues thought the same and he had to argue his point about why, despite the company's growth, they didn't need a complex expense policy. He then discovered Netflix's expenses, gift, entertainment and travel policy, which is 'act in Netflix's best interest'.[50] Five simple words that show significant autonomy and responsibility. Many would argue that this kind of policy isn't scalable, yet Netflix has shown that it works. In fact, as it has grown, Netflix has allowed *more* autonomy. Steve thought that needed to be Newicon's policy.

In a follow-up conversation, Steve explained to his fellow leaders, 'Sometimes, people want policy to save brain space, but most often, we hire people *for* their brains, for making smart decisions.'[51] He went on to talk about how Newicon has adopted a similar policy to Apple of giving 'fearless feedback'.[52] He said this 'leadership by copying other people is great leadership'.[53] Indeed, I hope this book allows you to do just that.

Another podcast guest who spoke firmly on the subject of giving away power is Mark Cuddigan, CEO of baby-food brand, Ella's Kitchen. Mark believes that leadership is a privilege and leaders need to serve and enable autonomy at work as their core role. He role-models this from the top: Mark gave up decision making altogether four years ago.

Practically, he says this is about stating and reinforcing to people that they are the experts. He is simply there as a sounding board who can offer his input if that's helpful, but he's not the final decision maker. He is firm on this. He goes on to share that if we take decision making away from people, this is really damaging. We must all consider the negative impact of withdrawing responsibility if we get the desire to take back to control.

Mark believes that autonomy allows your teams to align their work with their values. If your teams aren't empowered to make decisions, they can't enact your values. This is about the pride people have in the work they do. People who are enabled in this way can be proud of the active decisions they are making every day and the purpose that comes with that. More on the power of purpose later.

In terms of what holds leaders back from offering people autonomy, Mark believes, at least in more traditional settings, that it is inhibited by what they think leadership is about. Traditionally, people think it's about being able to 'tell people what to do', so for many, it's an opportunity to satisfy their own ego. Mark shares that this isn't what people who work for you want, nor will it give you fulfilment as a leader.

From an employee perspective, a resistance to taking on responsibility and decision making is often down to a lack of confidence. To deal with this, you need to help the person understand why they are feeling this way, employing great listening and understanding skills so they can move forward.

I would add that handing over control comes down to trust and clear intention. If your team members believe you deeply trust them to do the best they can, they will feel this and will be more likely to take on responsibility, which then builds confidence. A virtuous circle.

Patterns of behaviour around control are common among many of us, even the most progressive. The difference is that more progressive leaders are aware of these patterns. Again, self-awareness is the first step here.

You may experiment with letting go of control and find yourself reverting to a 'do it this way' approach because it gets the task done faster and is perhaps more endorphin-inducing. Congratulate yourself – you are at least noticing. From here, you can practise handing over control to your teams with certain projects or initiatives that arise and see what happens.

I interviewed Tom Tapper, the CEO of marketing agency Nice and Serious, who has a fantastic system for creating significant autonomy. Tom has a real passion for serving responsible business. He and his leadership team wanted to focus on charities or commercial clients with ethical causes, but they found they were taking on clients who were offering them projects that were at times a bit soulless. The staff felt that some of their work lacked significant morality. It was clear on occasions that the client just wanted to make as much money as possible and this wasn't why people had come to work for Nice and Serious. This issue needed solving.

The staff came up with a big idea after an away day. They suggested the company needed a meter by which the employees could vote on whether it should take on the client project or not. Less than 50% votes, the project would be refused.

The Moral Compass was born. It is released to employees every time a new project comes in and allows them to collectively make the call on whether it fits with their own morals. This is real staff empowerment to balance the company needs with the ethics of the project at hand. Impressive stuff.

Tom recognises that Nice and Serious can't pay the big bucks like some agencies, but what the teams can do is maintain meaningful work through their own collective discretion. This is powerful.

The highs and lows of autonomy

Let's not paint a rosy picture here; allowing more autonomy is not without its challenges. From my experience, a major challenge is around egos. If you provide a lot of autonomy, how do you stop employees getting too big for their boots?

This was a question I put to Daniel Hulme, who wants to provide as much freedom as is humanly possible in his artificial intelligence (AI) company, Satalia. In fact, he is striving for autonomy more than anyone I have met before. Managing this, he said, comes down to boundaries and accountability. Adults (like children) need boundaries; they provide a freedom to experiment and make decisions within certain parameters. They also need accountability; they need to be responsible.

Practically, this means giving people access to the maximum amount of information possible with the right systems in place for communication and reporting. This enables them to make good decisions and report to others in transparent ways. The result that Daniel sees is that people make much better decisions when empowered in this way.

Empowerment is about the right balance between authority and accountability. Daniel says, 'If you have lots of authority and no accountability, then you can do bad things, but if you have lots of accountability and no authority, then people can take advantage of you.'[54] For Daniel, it is a matter of human dignity to find this balance.

I have seen situations where people have had too much autonomy. Indeed, at one corporate where I worked, the culture was that of a high degree of autonomy. This worked for many (who, due to the sheer amount of freedom they'd experienced, found it difficult to work anywhere else), but for some, this was really difficult. A few felt that their seniors weren't interested in their work or that they were solitary. I certainly felt lonely and overwhelmed at times, but I did adapt.

I put my success in this organisation down to my manager. He taught me about the culture, which supported my growth. He also gave me a lot of responsibility at a young age. This meant I could achieve big things in my time with the company.

One example was designing and organising a major event as it moved around Europe. We hosted the event every year in collaboration with the local Ministry of Education in each place we visited. There would always be a speaker from the Ministry of Education and an executive from the company I worked for, but other than that, I had free rein to invite education speakers from all over the world as well as key delegates such as local experts and policy makers from around Europe.

My manager was involved somewhat in the planning of the events, but he was often travelling and gave me a lot of decision making to do about how to spend my time. Although he gave me a high degree of autonomy, he balanced that with a keen interest in what I was doing. He was always available for a chat, but he would often throw issues back my way to deal with.

It would no doubt have been a lot faster and easier in the short term for him to solve my problems for me, but he understood the value of autonomy. He was keen that I learn through making my own decisions. At times, this was brave; there were lots of senior stakeholders involved in the events and he delegated a huge amount to me.

For me, this showed his humility. He wasn't interested in getting the glory. He needed some visibility, yes, but he also wanted me to shine and grow as a person.

Developing a culture of autonomy

The work of a leader will involve both directive and nondirective approaches. The most directive is telling someone exactly what to do; the least directive (or most nondirective) approach is silence or 'witness'. Between the two, there are a huge range of styles involving things like summarising or paraphrasing someone else's words on the nondirective end to allow them to feel heard or offering a hypothesis or feedback on the more directive end.

What I see most leaders tend towards is the directive approach, the telling. We need to work at the nondirective end much more as this is where the transformational potential in our employees lies.

Of course, occasionally there is just cause to be extremely directive, perhaps due to issues of personal safety or legal protection when people need to follow clear instructions to the letter. In most roles, though, these situations are few and far between, so we need to practise the nondirective. This goes back to listening.

If we stay present for someone, holding our curiosity and sense of belief in them, they will often naturally solve problems for themselves. Others need more encouragement. Like control for some leaders, being told what to do is a comfort to certain team members, so while we as leaders need to learn to give autonomy, we also need to make sure employees build the confidence to take it. This is a practice.

When a more autonomous culture permeates a company, it's infectious.

Often, our employees impress us with the things they can do, now we have finally got out of the way. This links to the subject of purpose. If people are working in a way that suits them and driving change in a way that they think is relevant, they are more likely to find purpose in their work. Purpose is highly motivating.

 CASE STUDY: STAFF COUNCILS

EPISODE 15: THE CONSCIOUS LEADERS PODCAST

What Guy Singh-Watson, founder at Riverford, did was quite phenomenal in terms of giving away power: he moved Riverford to a governance structure of employee ownership.

Riverford puts a vast amount of responsibility into co-owner councils (staff councils to you and me). As a result, what Guy saw was not only the rise in motivation of people, but also a high degree of responsible decision making. Turns out that power in this way does not corrupt.

This was best illustrated when the council needed to decide the type of employee ownership the company would move to. Would employees have direct ownership, where they would have shares and could buy and sell them, or would the money be held in trust on behalf of employees (meaning they were only shareholders while they were employees of Riverford)? To Guy's amazement, the group decided on the latter.

This decision was significant for him because it was not one that would leave those who made it in the better situation. They would lose out financially if the money was held in trust for employees, yet the group decided that this was the best outcome for the organisation and for them as a collective.

When I interviewed Guy, it was clear how emotional this moment was for him. Guy had come from a background in the City, where working hard and fast was the name of the game. It seemed that this moment showed him what is possible when we do business differently.

Riverford did well out of the COVID-19 pandemic and at the time of interviewing (April 2021), the co-owner councils were deciding how to spend this windfall. They could provide it all as dividends for employees, but the decision looked like it was heading towards an equal share going into funding environmental initiatives. The co-owners recognise that Riverford as an organisation needs to look long and hard at itself to interrogate its own environmental impact. In this way, employees can enact their collective values for good.

For me, I can't think of a better example of autonomy in action. Responsible business at its finest.

KEY TAKEAWAYS

- The main barrier to *giving away* power is our need for control.

- Control is unsustainable and it doesn't allow for ownership or the resultant fulfilment at work.

- The main barriers to *taking* responsibility are trust and confidence.

- For autonomy to work effectively, we need the right balance between authority and accountability.

PRACTICAL WAYS TO GIVE AWAY POWER

- Implement a strong and clear intention to provide enhanced trust and confidence among employees.

- Decentralise and create smaller, more autonomous teams.

- Experiment with giving up decision making for a set period.

- Use democratic systems around key decisions or general governance.

- Implement employee-ownership models.

10
Lesson 6: Build a sense of safety

Feeling safe at work is an interesting concept, one that we may or may not have been aware of. We will certainly remember if we have experienced the opposite: where the environment was unsafe; where we felt the need to watch our backs and cover our tracks repeatedly for fear of being caught out, criticised or reprimanded in some way. Perhaps we felt the fear of having done something wrong and not wanting to own up to this fact or admit our involvement; a 'he said, she said' culture where people may have been pitted against each other, even in subtle ways.

One thing is for sure, you can't just declare an environment 'safe'; you need to build it, earn it.

Those in it are the only ones who can tell you if they feel safe.

One podcast guest who was really intentional about this is Charlotte Williams of influencer marketing agency SevenSix. I interviewed Charlotte on the day she moved into the agency's new office space in Soho (something that speaks of her easy-going nature in itself).

Charlotte said that the biggest hope for her was her employees would feel 'both safe and happy';[55] that it would be awful to think anyone would experience a 'Monday dread' feeling. At the time of interviewing, the teams were just starting to unpack the boxes at their office, which she said she wanted to 'feel like their second home': somewhere they could invite their friends after work and make use of the fully stocked bar. For the young people working at her agency, I bet this is the kind of leader they want: someone who trusts them and wants them to feel safe and at home.

One foundational trait I found in leaders around whom people feel safe is consistency. This is particularly relevant to the self-management of our moods and how we handle difficult situations.

You may recall in 'Lesson 2: Actively manage yourself' (Chapter 6), we talked about mirror neurons and the dramatic impact that our mood has on others. This plays acutely into people feeling safe at work too. Even if we walk into a room without saying much, people will detect our mood and many will be affected by it.

Clearly, this means we need to work through our issues and not lash out at others or display random acts of venting. This does not mean that we shouldn't have our own safe space for this – being able to express our emotions can be cathartic, just in the right context.

People around us will respond well to processed emotion – difficulties that we have somewhat worked through with a confidant or a coach. June Cory spoke of this in our interview. She reported that for people who she previously would not have been able to predict how they would react, processed emotion worked well. For her, it's the same.

She says, 'I'm always a bit manic and always positive.'[56] She is self-aware enough to know that not everyone may have (or know how to handle) the same level of enthusiasm she has. At times, she holds back, but she's keen that she brings her positivity and that people know to expect that.

At the root of this, your employees want to feel your stability. It doesn't mean you have to be superhuman. In fact, your vulnerability – in terms of the emotions you have actively processed, along with the story of the journey you have been on – will warm people to you. It's your day-to-day moods that need to be managed.

Managing my own reactivity wasn't something that used to be easy for me at all. In my early to mid-twenties, I had quite a temper. It wasn't until later, when I started working on my own development with a coach and through training in mindfulness, that I saw my behaviour change. With that, my reactivity reduced. I saw how my behaviour could slow down so I had a choice about how to respond in a way that was more skilful. It's about regaining our freedom to choose how to respond, especially in moments of high stress which test us the most.

John Hesler, the former 'tough guy' from construction, now meditates twice a day for twenty minutes a time. He said that he wouldn't be without this practice as it supports him in the way he behaves with his two young children and four companies. Even his dad is meditating now, which John said he wouldn't have thought would happen in his wildest dreams.

Podcast guest Susan Glenholme, managing partner at a law firm, said that she has always taught employees in her company to know that 'if you do well, you'll get the credit, but if you do badly, the buck stops with leadership'.[57] In other words, if employees don't know the right thing to do, it's probably because the leaders didn't train them well enough. She reports that 'people feel quite bad if they mess up in some way, so we don't have to make it worse for them'.[58] What a refreshing approach: a real safety net to catch employees in their workplace, particularly in a sector like law where I have witnessed the opposite on a few occasions.

Grace Francis is a chief experience officer for Accenture Song (part of consulting giant, Accenture) and identifies as nonbinary, something they are keen to talk about (more on that in Chapter 11 on equal belonging). Grace works in a high-pressure industry. Consequently, we ended up discussing what happens when people struggle at work and their performance dips. Grace reports that people can feel quite panicky – then they stop being able to engage their brain. For example, this can happen when people receive feedback, eg that they are not a good listener, in a public arena. This feedback may be well intended, but if it isn't delivered with much EQ, it can end up making people feel stressed and inadequate.

It may be that a project has stalled or a pitch has failed. People can take extreme amounts of personal responsibility for this, ending up with a dialogue in their heads that says, 'I should have worked harder...' or 'If I had done one thing better...' Grace reports that such a 'failure' is never down to one thing and is just an integral part of the nature of business.

For Grace, support looks like taking the pressure away for a period of time so people have a chance to 'catch their breath and recentre themselves'. They said that one benefit of the COVID-19 pandemic was that it became easier to share needs around wellbeing. Consulting can be intense and a window of space allows people to 'remember how capable they are'.[59] I love the depth of Grace's intention here.

Project Aristotle at Google

Google did some interesting research called 'Project Aristotle'.[60] It sought to find out what made some teams, internally to Google, more high-performing than others. What was the difference that made the difference? In this way, Google could share the results internally with the way it leads its people and externally as a thought leader in the wider business world.

The results were not what the company leaders expected. There were various hypotheses about what makes a high-performing team – was it a particular mix of introverts and extroverts? People who get along outside of work? A certain balance of personality types? What the results showed was that the key determining factor in high-performing teams is psychological safety, demonstrated in two key ways.

The first is emotional awareness – how aware the team members are of each other. This points to how in tune they are with each other's differences and needs generally, and how aware they are of the other person and their needs on a particular day.

One method that Pip Jamieson instigated at The Dots was a randomised paired coffee catch-up each week, enabling colleagues to have a thirty-minute nonwork meeting and get to know each other more fully. This simple method is a fantastic way to build internal relationships and reduce isolation, especially in dispersed teams. It means that staff get to know more about their colleagues as real people, which enables them to be more emotionally aware of each other.

Simple practices that I introduce to clients to use at the beginning of a meeting include a check-in. This can help gauge how the individuals of the group are doing. I suggest doing this as a weather pattern exercise. One person leads and invites everyone to shut their eyes and take a good thirty seconds to one minute to scan their body from top to toe, noticing the weather pattern. Without comment or interruption, they then go round and invite people to state their weather pattern. It could be 'bright blue skies' or 'tornadoes', but it gives a clearer indication of how people are than a stock 'fine'.

A lot of this stuff is really simple, but it does take a little time to do. It's much more adrenaline-inducing to steam on with a meeting. The weather pattern exercise is a moment of taking our foot off the accelerator, which means people can settle in and be more comfortable knowing they are accepted just as they are. It also allows us to follow up later with individuals without them feeling like they have to explain themselves during a meeting.

The second key factor of psychological safety, according to Project Aristotle's results, is equality in conversational turn-taking. In other words, everyone has equal time to speak.

This has a couple of benefits. There is equality of opportunity as everyone feels heard and that they have a say in the discussion and decision making. The other is that it allows you as a leader to unearth key knowledge that may be going untapped. Perhaps the individuals in a team who don't generally speak up have great ideas which would help you move your projects forward with more efficiency and fun. Often, the quieter ones are more observational; they have time to study the wider aspects of what is going on, but they stay quiet and you lose their knowledge. Unwittingly (or sometimes completely consciously) others drown them out or bulldoze over them.

There are many simple methods for creating more equality in meetings. One method is introduced by Nancy Kline in her great book called *Time to Think*.[61] She recommends nine guidelines of chairing brilliant meetings, which include a focus on appreciation at the beginning and end, allowing each person to speak and the rest of the group to listen without judgement. Interrupting is not allowed; Nancy Kline says that people think faster and say more without interruption.

By focusing on appreciation, we cultivate the ability within our teams to listen to each person in turn. This simple method is powerful as it allows people to feel heard and contribute in an equitable way. Try it.

It also has a cumulative effect as those who were less likely to contribute now have more practice in doing just that. Hopefully, they then gain more confidence, especially if their ideas are being recognised by the group. It is all too easy to listen to the loud, charismatic team members, but the ones displaying a clumsy unrehearsed genius may be those we need to step up.

Focusing on appreciation only works when we apply the methods of listening we discussed earlier in the book. To implement these methods, we have a choice: we could explain the system to our teams or we could simply role model it without drawing too much attention to it and let it play out.

It may be helpful to offer the group a simple prompt before you start focusing on appreciation, such as:

'We will go round and contribute in turn for two to three minutes to help solve this particular problem. Instead of planning what you will say during other people's turns, see what it is like to listen and practise being present, bringing your attention back each time it wanders. This mind-wandering is natural; it's just what minds do, so return to focus each time, knowing that when it is your turn, you can see what pops up.'

Alternatively, use your own version.

A speak-up culture

By developing an environment where people know that it is safe to speak up, you will get more breadth of confidence and creativity in your team. It is likely that motivation will also rise as people take on more ownership by contributing their ideas.

Megan Reitz is a professor from Ashridge Business School as well as a facilitator, coach and author I look up to in this field. Reitz's research says that 'this [a speak-up culture] is often less about the less powerful having a voice and more about the more powerful really wanting to listen to others throughout the organisation'.[62] Reitz highlights to leaders that they may not realise how scary they are to employees, thereby inhibiting them from sharing information. Often, she finds that leaders think they are receptive to others, citing an 'open door policy' or that they are simply 'approachable', but her research shows that this is one of the biggest blind spots for leaders.[63]

She's also quick to highlight our biases as leaders – that, consciously or unconsciously, we may have a little 'book of troublemakers' to whom we roll our eyes or don't listen as soon as they speak.[64] It's something to watch out for, as we may only hear information from a few perspectives, which silences a whole group who we have deemed to have nothing useful to add. Again, this could be unconscious.

Nick Heap, who we met in Chapter 7, reported that a senior colleague of his often repeated the question 'If I were a great idea, where would I hide?' and the answer was 'In the mind of a junior member of staff who's watching and listening'. We need to be aware of our blind spots for favouring and sidestepping people in organisations. This facilitates the sharing of information, great ideas and the swell of learning and growth in our teams.

We may also find that the 'difficult' ones in our teams can turn out to be some of the most helpful contributors. Quite often, no one is listening to them, so they get louder and louder in their disgruntled nature and perhaps less and less effective in their communication method. In reality, these people are putting a lot of effort into their objections – they clearly care.

In the past, they might have been written off as awkward. It's interesting the difference that we can make to them with a bit of attention and listening, especially if concurrently, we stamp out any gossiping going on about them.

KEY TAKEAWAYS

- Our employees feeling safe at work starts with consistency and the stability of our mood as a leader.

- In 'Project Aristotle', Google found the success of high-performing teams was 'psychological safety' and that comprised of two key elements:

  1. Emotional awareness

  2. Equality in conversational turn-taking

PRACTICAL WAYS TO BUILD A SENSE OF SAFETY

- Have your own external confidant or coach with whom you can work through your difficulties. Employees will respond well to your processed emotion.

- Provide a safety net for employees to fail. Your title comes with responsibility.

- Encourage more personal relationships between everyone (as opposed to natural cliques) such as randomised coffee catch-ups.

- Check in with people's 'weather pattern' at the beginning of a meeting.

- Build in routine listening exercises to create more equality and creativity. No interrupting – watch the magic happen.

- Reflect on any troublemakers or favourites lists you have – the awkward ones can transform when you listen and believe in them.

11
Lesson 7: Foster a sense of equal belonging

The previous chapters all contribute to a sense of belonging, but I feel that it needs calling out separately as it is a conscious and systemic process that leads to equal belonging. From my interviews, it appears fundamental to successful teams.

I say equal belonging as opposed to just belonging because otherwise, we end up with some groups feeling like they belong more than others. This points directly to the irony of *Animal Farm* by George Orwell: 'All animals are equal, but some animals are more equal than others'.[65] Belonging includes everyone. This environment doesn't have cliques and gossip. These things are stamped out repeatedly to preserve a fertile environment for growth.

Belonging also points to a mode of service from a leader. Instead of wanting to take the glory or wield their own ego, often the leaders I interview see how they can support and serve those around them to create an environment of belonging. In this chapter, I'll look at the way leaders manage themselves in this mode of service before moving on to the cultural or systemic methods.

Servant leadership

Servant leadership is a well-documented approach. Robert K Greenleaf coined the phrase in 1970, describing it as the 'aspiration to lead… driven by a desire to serve others'.[66] In his essay 'The servant as leader', Greenleaf explained, 'A servant-leader focuses primarily on the growth and well-being of people and the communities to which they belong.' People in positions of authority are uniquely equipped to take on this role, but how many do it?

One of the best podcast guests for enacting service and belonging is Jean Baptiste Oldenhove, founder of Estari Group. His motivation links to Lesson 1 on intention: he is keen that he always goes into a meeting with employees or external people with an intention of 'How can I help you?' For him to help others, he needs to listen and use some of the methods mentioned in the previous chapter to build a sense of safety. He is particularly keen on grounding and recommends this mode of attitude to the others in his staff. To him, these are foundational behaviours for life and work.

As someone who runs an investment company, Jean Baptiste reports that many entrepreneurs do not really listen to investors or serve them in the right way. They want to go in fast and pitch themselves and wow the investors, but they forget that, while the other person may have an impressive history, they are also just a human being.

Human beings want to be listened to; they want to be understood. If there is common understanding, then both the investor and the entrepreneur can work together and feel like they belong together to solve the challenge that their business supports.

Another leader who embodies service and belonging really well is Susan Glenholme, managing partner at law firm Debenhams Ottaway. Susan worked her way up from the bottom as a trainee solicitor, all the way to the top. She is still at the same firm twenty-four years on.

She reports that she was always given opportunities as a junior and treated well. Indeed, she was brought up by her employer to believe she could make it to the top, and she seeks to translate and enhance that in her leadership tenure. She loves managing others, their different personality styles, helping them manage their potential.

She sees herself as a custodian of the business: that it is her job to run the firm responsibly and hand it to the next generation in a healthy state. This translates in terms of her responsibility to serve employees and help them fulfil their potential. She will listen as keenly to a trainee as she will to a senior staff member, recognising that people want to feel heard and be happy at work. If she can practically help people be happier at work, she'll do it.

Her ability to give equal value to junior and senior members of staff provides a sense of fairness and belonging as people all feel valued and part of something. Indeed, to build on this in terms of culture development, Susan talks frequently about 'one team' at Debenhams Ottaway. Everyone has a collective duty to serve people and help each other out. She expects that if something needs doing, employees will pick it up. People at all levels need to get their hands dirty.

Her company is not a place for egos and individuals; it's a collective culture. She sees the commercial benefits of this too – employees can easily cross-refer clients at her law firm from property to wills to family law; there is plenty of opportunity for people to cross-pollinate, so she sees benefit in a collective culture from both the overall wellbeing of employees and the business.

The anonymous ex-leader from technology in banking – the one I called Jocelyn – who I spoke about near the beginning of the book had a winning department of forty people, which was the envy of the rest of the company. She put it down to the strength of the collective relationships, which resulted in group socials, people actively seeking each other out for support and lots of comradery around common problems.

I asked her how she fostered this type of environment and she reported that it was by giving everyone an equal voice. She said that no one person's title was more important than anyone else's. Everyone felt valued equally and she encouraged the personal conversations and connections.

Some bosses think that when people are chatting while at work, they are somehow skiving off. As long as there is a good work ethic broadly, what they are actually doing is building relationships, which means they are more likely to support each other in times of need.

Helen Gillett, now COO at BetterSpace (managing director at Affinity for Business at the time of interviewing), reported how she invited *everyone* to the offsite company strategy sessions. She said these strategy days were not for the privileged few to sit in a posh hotel room and drink posh coffee, but about everyone having the opportunity to be included. Some people found this quite strange as they'd never been included in strategy conversations, but what it brought was better thinking.

'You get ideas that you wouldn't have got otherwise,' Helen told me.[67] She said she still has live conversations in her head about belonging and how to make workplaces inclusive. This is an iterative journey for Helen.

I have frequently facilitated inclusive offsite vision building and strategy sessions over one or two days for companies, with a treasured colleague of mine called Phil Walsh. Phil has complementary skills to mine – he's great at ramping up the energy and I'm better at grounding people. Together, we're a force for good.

What is interesting about the way leaders tend to plan offsite meetings is they think employees need a ton of updates, slides and training. These meetings are actually about asking ourselves, 'How do we want people to feel when they leave?' Often, people want to feel empowered and involved, and have some time to socialise and build stronger connections. This builds emotional awareness, which is key for psychological safety and subsequent high-performing teams.

People want to feel valued and that they are part of creating something. Yes, there might be some updates, but we can weave these into a strategy session. In fact, if we let people speak, they're likely to come up with the same if not better ideas than senior leaders. Plus, they'll be motivated to take them forward while senior leadership share the glory, the ownership. *This* makes for impactful leadership.

Phil and I always take briefings from the senior leadership team to talk about the key goals for an offsite event. Next, we work to create an employee-centred day which includes what people have experienced and what they've learnt (highs and lows) before moving on to building a vision with practical action plans to follow.

It's hugely important to allow people to acknowledge the past before moving forward. I found this particularly pertinent as we were coming out of the COVID-19 pandemic. We didn't need to dwell there, but we did need to honour it to enable people to move forward in committed ways.

The great thing for senior leaders is that they don't need to do much on the day except be part of the fun. As long as we are conscious of their needs, they trust us. We do things like allowing people to present their vision in creative ways, develop core ideas, and then anonymously and democratically vote on which ideas to take forward. The feedback is always hugely positive. People feel heard and included, not just in the content, but in the way we run the day.

People come to strategy days with needs and ideas. Often, leaders stamp these out of them and they go home exhausted and overwhelmed.

Let's use these days to motivate and empower people so they are ready to drive the next steps for us. Let's give them this voice.

A podcast guest who allows a strong employee voice in a large organisation is Phil Wild, CEO at James Cropper. After he had done an investigation into the best way to empower people through values, the organisational leaders stripped down their values by going back to the drawing board and running a six-month-long process of understanding how their employees understood who they were.

In a business of over 600 employees, this process involved a cross-section from a range of seniorities, geographies, ages and genders participating in workshops to enable the values to be distilled. The executive team needed to double-down on listening as a key skill. They participated in the workshops, but did not say much. In doing so, they ensured that the company values (forward thinking, responsible and caring) are owned by employees.

This is what belonging feels like. I'm particularly impressed that an organisation of this size undertook this kind of thorough process. Phil was open about the fact that the values would have been created much more quickly in one workshop in a boardroom; they just would have been meaningless to everyone else.

James Cropper's values are made real by its teams' support of the Teenage Cancer Trust and their initiative to refurbish some of the company's un-used buildings to house Ukrainian refugees escaping from the Russian invasion in 2022. The latter example came from employees who wanted to volunteer their time to support these refugees. This sounds like empowered employees living their values and getting their employer to step up alongside them.

Diversity and inclusion

To take a broad perspective on belonging and race, let's move back to Helen Gillett. Her interview took place soon after the murder of George Floyd and the rise of the Black Lives Matter movement in 2020. She said that she, in hindsight, had been complacent about race; she is now much more purposeful and active in her nonexecutive director roles to help 'amplify voices that don't get heard'.[68]

She admits that while Affinity for Business is quite a diverse organisation in terms of race and gender, the leadership team was all white. For her, this was the next phase of her learning to enhance inclusion. We spoke together about social mobility and access to opportunity and her words were, 'How do we open doors to people that don't even know these doors exist?' This speaks of an antiracist who is proactively looking at how to get different people around the table.

This down-to-earth collective responsibility pays dividends. Podcast guest and CEO, Ciaron Dunne, says he expects people to step up to big things, but he also expects everyone to go and pick up rubbish from the car park if Genie Ventures has an important visitor. There is something significant here about reducing egos and keeping everyone together and grounded.

To continue with perspectives on race and belonging, the person with whom I have spoken who has the deepest and most useful insights in this area is Shanice Mears (or Shannie as she likes to be known). I met her through her co-founder, Dan Saxby: together, Shannie and Dan run an advertising agency called The Elephant Room, which 'builds inclusive brands'.

Shannie believes that diversity and inclusion initiatives can be well intentioned but limited in their impact. Tactical actions such as having a broader range of people of colour in job adverts and undertaking unconscious bias training are great steps in the right direction, but what they lack is giving a diverse range of a people a seat at the top table. She notices from her black peers that many are in good jobs – ones that pay well, ones that contain interesting work – but they are not committed to them long term.

For Shannie, belonging is for the long term. For that to happen, people need to be given significant autonomy and knowledge of how they can grow. Shannie says, 'Belonging is one step further – it isn't about making me comfortable; it's about making me uncomfortable so that I can be the best person I can be.'[69]

This is a thought-provoking statement. From her perspective, inclusion isn't about wrapping people in cotton wool so that everyone feels comfortable; it's about stretching people and getting them to add their individual stamp to things through enabling them to have responsibility.

In my follow-up conversation with Hephzi Pemberton, founder of Equality Group, she said, 'It's about knowing what success looks like for someone' to support their growth.[70] In most situations, we should be able to satisfy both the employee's needs and those of the business. Hephzi is keen that Equality Group takes an iterative approach to employees' development, checking in as much as possible.

For her, that is a minimum of quarterly objective and key results (OKR) reviews, preferably more regularly than that in one-to-one catch-ups. She is keen this is an ongoing conversation about how to maximise growth. Hephzi recognises that the annual review, without in-between touchpoints, is simply out of date.

The benefit of a system like OKRs is that it gets really specific about our objectives and *how* we know we are meeting them (what would we be seeing, hearing, knowing?) and what initiatives will be happening (what would we be doing?). You can find simple templates for OKRs online.

Hephzi's company is a diversity and inclusion strategic consultancy, which makes her an authority on the subjects of inclusion and belonging, but she appears rather humble about it. In our interview, she told me how she seeks to practise what she preaches, working to role model diversity and inclusion for clients as much as serve them as a consultant.

In Hephzi's book *The Diversity Playbook*, she shares how she has worked on herself as a leader.[71] This includes doing an audit of her inner circle, something she recommends as an exercise to readers. She describes our inner circle as the top five people in our life who we trust and confide in (minus our partner and close family members). Hephzi recommends listing them and plotting their diversity demographics such as age, gender, sexuality, race, socio-economic group and disability.

When she originally did this exercise, she noticed that she had mainly educated women in their mid-thirties, similar to her, in her inner circle. She said, 'I had work to do on gender, age, disability and racial equality.' It didn't stop there. As Hephzi expanded her network to a broader group, she recognised the significance of the people in it to help steer her organisation. Equality Group's advisory board was born.

'It was built with the knowledge that diverse boards make better decisions,' said Hephzi in her book. This is something I have always respected about her. She advocates both the commercial and ethical reasons for this work and their clients' uses a strategic data-driven approach.

Many corporate leaders will need hard bottom-line benefits to drive change. Hephzi's organisation is fantastic at making the case for diversity so that it can be a core part of their clients' business strategy.

For Hephzi, creating belonging is about a feeling – one of being connected, respected, seen and heard. Indeed, connection is a word that came up frequently in our follow-up conversation. Hephzi says she means connection to many things, including colleagues to each other, to clients and to the overall vision and purpose of the company.

I particularly like the way Hephzi instigates the rotating of the role of chair in a meeting. This format pops up in many instances, including weekly team meetings as well as the board meeting. When she is not chair at the board meeting, Hephzi dedicates a bit more preparation time between her and whoever is hosting. Time she is keen to give. For Hephzi, she sees the advantages to the board to mix up the styles and allow other people to take more responsibility.

Equality Group's team meetings show further connection and belonging through how the teams set them up. The rotating chair for each week is asked to find and distribute a quote, reflection or image that they have found in some way inspiring or useful in advance of the meeting. The meeting then starts with a silent meditation of two minutes followed by a short discussion of whatever the chair shared.

This is an exceptional way to start both a meeting and a week. All too often, we as leaders come steaming into meetings feeling like we're spinning too many plates, particularly in a virtual set up where we are having back-to-back meetings. The constant switching of topics and people can be exhausting. This moment of stillness and reflection allows a broader perspective on life before the day-to-day business is covered. It's inclusive as different people will bring a different slant and tone each week, allowing others to share what is meaningful to them and get to know their colleagues better.

The power of pausing

From my experience of running short meditation practices at the beginning of meetings, I know the impact can be huge. If we are open to it, a simple meditation practice can allow us to arrive in mind as well as body and our sense of urgency to relax. From this point, we can make better decisions.

There is good neuroscientific evidence to back this up. Harvard Medical School conducted studies on participants in eight-week mindfulness courses (weekly sessions plus a daily meditation practice) which showed increases in grey matter in the hippocampus of the brain.[72] This is where we experience learning and memory and structures associated with self-awareness and compassion.[73] The research is conclusive: it is possible to rewire our brain through meditation to have greater EQ, but we will need proper commitment to a regular meditation practice to make this a reality.

Research from Hult Ashridge Executive Business School, led by Michael Chaskalson, has shown that leaders practising meditation for as little as ten minutes a day over the long term are more adaptable and will see significant increases in empathy and self-regulation,[74] but (there is a big 'but') most of the neurological changes don't start happening until around week five of the course. The point is that meditation may not give you a positive feedback loop for a while, so it's important to stick with it and trust the process. Like most things, the more you put in, the more you will get out, so finding a balance that works for you will be important.

Enable growth through belonging

Unlike Hephzi's organisation, which enables growth in others skilfully, many small businesses find it harder to enable growth than large organisations. This is usually because leaders emphasise the limits of opportunity within a small business.

While I see the merits of a reality check, the opportunities are different for small businesses. Because employees often don't have sight of a career ladder, opportunity can feel restricted, but this asks for more creative ways to help people grow without changing their job title.

For me, the career ladder model is limited in itself. When employees are always wishing they were at the next level, they can lose sight of actually getting good at what they are doing now. If there is a mis-fit with the role, that's different, but many people are too impatient to move up. In a small business environment (or flat corporate environment), we as leaders can show people how breadth of experience can support their long-term career aspirations.

This does need to be equitable. People spot unfairness in an instant. It asks the question, 'What culture are we creating in our organisation around growth?'

When I worked for the corporate that allowed employees a large amount of autonomy, we all picked our own job title, wrote our own job descriptions and agreed our objectives in ways that met both our personal and business needs. This was a relatively flat corporate culture and meant that we as employees gained a feeling of lateral growth and breadth of experience that was rewarding. Plus, people were less concerned about status as most were only about three to five degrees of separation from the CEO anyway. We didn't feel like there was an inner circle in power, something I've felt in many other organisations.

Back to Shannie of marketing agency, The Elephant Room, who witnesses a range of levels of ambition from her clients. Each client wants to create a sense of belonging with their customers because they are consumer brands and brand loyalty pays dividends.

At one end of the spectrum, Shannie reports, an organisation has completely dismantled its team. The organisation's leaders haven't fired anyone, but they've realised that some of the make-up of a particular team needed to change in terms of perspective and demographics for them to reach a young black-culture audience.

To create a true sense of belonging with customers, through their work with Shannie and others at The Elephant Room, the employees of this organisation realised that this needed to start at home. Consequently, Shannie has been working through a range of content each month with them so they can become aligned and focused on their goals. To make this practical, she shared how these workshops are themed around the topics of 'purpose, power, point, perspective, play and community'. In them, she facilitates the employees becoming clear on where they stand on these topics and how they want to behave.

Conversely, a few organisational leaders that Shannie works with are not that ambitious. They are not willing to do the internal work first that will allow them to reach their clients in more meaningful ways. Shannie is keen to get away from having too many meetings which don't address the core source of bias and discrimination. For her, if an organisation's leaders want to create belonging and community with their customers, the work will always be limited if it doesn't start at home.

Grace Francis, the chief experience officer for Accenture Song, is someone who enables belonging through shifting the dynamic in the room. Grace has been in human-centred creative spaces for many years and has a deep interest in the human experience. They demonstrate true leadership in the space of belonging by, for example, often entering a group of twenty people they don't know at work and declaring that they are nonbinary. They make a bit of a joke about it and offer the opportunity for anyone to speak to them afterwards.

Grace thinks that it's a gift to offer their difference so that others might feel more comfortable with theirs. Their intention here is really strong.

In our follow-up conversation to our interview, Grace said, 'I bring my confidence and in doing so, share that confidence with others – you can't do anything wrong in this room.'[75]

What an empowering place to be. This speaks significantly of the aspect of safety, a subject we covered earlier. I haven't known Grace for long, but I have to say I felt remarkably comfortable in their company in quite an instantaneous way. Their belonging capacity is palpable and it helps people thrive.

For Grace, belonging is about the merge between personal and professional. If something huge is going on for you personally, it may be difficult for you to concentrate. This can also apply to world events such as the invasion of Ukraine by Russia or the murdering of black people by police in the United States. If those world issues are personal to you, you may need to discuss them in the workplace.

To bring this to life, when Grace worked in a radio station, one of their quiet colleagues suddenly let out a scream of horror. It became apparent that the lady's brother had been killed in South Africa. Before they knew it, the whole radio station organically found out what she needed and acted on it.

Someone took over her show; someone called round to find out information; someone else found her the space she needed and so on. This wasn't just one-off help; in the days, weeks and months that followed, there was a lot of consideration given to her and the grief she was experiencing. She was allowed to mourn and take the time she needed over the long term.

Grace said, 'Work is a construct and because we are always busy, we can flip that to being never busy. Sometimes, we just need to stop.'[76]

This sentiment was echoed by podcast guest Clair Heaviside. Clair is co-founder of a young and dynamic marketing agency in Manchester, UK called Serotonin that recently won an award for Best Small Digital Agency in the Northern Digital Awards. Clair acknowledges that people are multifaceted and complex. If we want someone to be successful in their career, we need to address the whole of their self and not just the professional part of them.

She said that at Serotonin, there's a culture where talking about anxiety, depression or sadness is as simple and open as talking about anything else. She firmly believes that this needs to start with the leadership, who have created a culture of being yourself. If she can be herself and talk openly and normalise what's going on in her life, then others can do the same and feel part of a supportive environment.

Back to Grace Francis: they understand belonging as well as any other by identifying as nonbinary. They don't feel that they fit into the female groups, nor the necessarily male groups. I asked about how companies support people transitioning, trans or nonbinary. Grace said it is important to offer training and open conversations, but also not to expect people to 'come out' as they may or may not be ready to do that at work. The door needs to be open and people should see that by how we as leaders engage with other diverse groups and how inclusive we are of other people's differences, be they religious, ethnicity, sexuality or disability based. Each interaction here is a moment for us to build a space of belonging.

I recently listened to a podcast interview by Tim Ferriss with Ben Horowitz.[77] Ben was a bit of a big cheese in the early days of Silicon Valley and beyond. He worked for companies such as Netscape, AOL and HP and during that time, he learnt a lot about change management in the buying and selling of companies through volatile conditions.

It is interesting he has gone on to focus on leadership and culture himself in his writing: his latest book is called *What You Do Is Who You Are: How to create your business culture.*[78] He talks about culture being built steadily by day-to-day actions. You can easily build upon a culture of belonging and enact it in ways such as listening circles around inclusion and belonging topics, ones which include everyone.

For Grace, the future of inclusivity is being open to those of privilege too. One of the biggest transformations they've seen is from a white man who went to Eton.

'He was told to hide his past, change his trainers and make his name more working class [to fit into a creativity culture],' Grace told me.[79] Grace allowed him to be who he was and share the benefits and limitations of that. In doing so, they enabled him to develop an enhanced capacity to include others.

White men can be (consciously or unconsciously) excluded from diversity conversations, yet the reality is that they still hold the majority of the board and C-Suite positions of power and influence. If we don't listen to those in privileged positions, then we can't collaborate.

Grace said, 'No one wants to be told they are doing something wrong,' so we need to be open to everyone.[80] Saying something doesn't go far enough; we need to show it so people feel it's everyone's place to be part of the conversation.

In reflecting on this work, I have realised how segregated a lot of our inclusion work can be. Of course, there can be benefits to that in a sense of similarity or togetherness, but I'm wondering if something bigger is lost in that we aren't bringing everyone with us. Belonging, like wellbeing, is a bottom-line conversation and should be held at the highest levels of a company, not delegated to small groups with low budgets and one-off activities. Despite a lot of goodwill and talk, we need to work harder for this to happen effectively.

KEY TAKEAWAYS

- Belonging starts with a mode of service as a leader.

- Belonging is about long-term commitment to your organisation. Every moment is an opportunity to build belonging. Those who feel different will watch how you handle others who feel different.

- Belonging that allows long-term commitment will come from people feeling their growth is supported.

- Ask yourself:

  - How can personal or world events be supported in the workplace? This is a huge opportunity to step up for people.

  - How can I help people create their own career growth in the organisation, one that allows them to bring their personal values and strengths?

  - How do the other leaders and I make inclusion conversations not exclusive in themselves, but part of the core business strategy? Inclusion makes for better business.

PRACTICAL WAYS TO BUILD A SENSE OF BELONGING

- Stamp out individualistic behaviours and build a collective culture, one that means people at all levels get their hands dirty. If they work as a collective, they will be more likely to support each other in personal and professional ways.

- Provide an opportunity for everyone to have a voice, eg by sharing your attention across seniority levels, inclusive employee-centred company offsite meetings and regular listening circles.

12
Lesson 8: Let people in

Emotional awareness as one of the key traits in high-performing teams (referencing Chapter 10 on safety) involves the ability for leaders to open up about the difficult times. Some call this vulnerability. This I find quite a polarising word, particularly, if I'm generalising, for men.

If you haven't been allowed to be vulnerable, particularly as a child and in social circles, it might be rather tough to call on your vulnerability now, especially on-demand. Those who are into vulnerability tend to get excited and want us all to share open-heartedly, while those who aren't want to run away in the opposite direction at the speed of light. Because it is so polarising, vulnerability should be handled with great care.

That said, we mustn't avoid it. It is a delicate balance.

What this is *really* about is the power
of connection, which can emerge
when we share something personal.

Let me be clear: this is not an easy path for many leaders, including the guests on the podcast, but it is one that has the most remarkable effects. Leaders are all on their own journey and take different approaches to openness.

This kind of openness is built upon the traits we've already discussed, which is why the topic comes so far into the book. We can't possibly expect openness if we don't first build the environment to accommodate it, but it can emerge when we do.

The reason that I've picked out this trait is that it has had one of the largest instantaneous ripple effects I have ever seen. Whole levels of new connection and commitment can emerge, I would go so far as to say, overnight.

Show your vulnerability as your strength

Whatever your vulnerability is, it needs to be authentic. Authenticity is another word that can sometimes be unhelpful. As soon as we *try* to be authentic, we've lost our authenticity. True authenticity emerges over time with self-awareness, feelings of safety and confidence and a comfort with who we are – just as we are, with all our imperfections.

I'll go first. In autumn 2020, I experienced a huge change in my life: I left my husband for a woman. It was a challenging time which left me wrought with anxiety and guilt, as well as the positive emotions of love and care I had for my new partner. I had to dig deep to have difficult conversations about the way I felt as my feelings emerged. I didn't cheat, but I mentally cheated and when I couldn't get her out of my head, I had to be open about it.

The biggest thing for me was that it was a huge risk. Becky, my current partner, and I hadn't flirted with each other at all; we'd just spent time together and connected. We were two women who thought they were straight (I need to write a whole book on that alone, to be honest), so I took a gamble by opening up about the way I felt to my husband.

I was scared as tirades of negative thought would come steaming into my meditations and daily life: 'Am I a terrible person?'; 'Am I doing the wrong thing?'; 'Maybe I'm messing it all up right now'. The negativity bias of the brain was playing on a loud-speaker night and day.

I had a lot of therapy at that time. I was processing a huge amount of emotion after being with my husband for twelve years. It was a good marriage, not a bad one; I had just found something so profound that I couldn't not act on it.

To cut a long story short, being labelled as 'gay' has been OK for me (although I would regard myself as bisexual). Besides those close to me, I'm not too worried what people think of me and I feel lucky to be living in a country where the rights and understanding of gay people are so progressive. I know that's not the same for everyone.

That's me being open. I don't hide my sexuality; I make a point of saying 'My partner, *she…*' because it normalises it for everyone. The more people talk openly, the more society changes and is accepting of different types of people.

What did I learn through that period? That being honest and talking openly is important. Anxiety is normal, the most understandable emotion for the period, and working through it without being rash or reactive was the right thing to do. I learnt that it is OK to hold lots of emotions together at once – grief, love, anxiety, loss, excitement. One emotional rollercoaster.

CASE STUDY: CONNECTING THROUGH SHARED GRIEVING

EPISODE 22: THE CONSCIOUS LEADERS PODCAST

Mark Cuddigan, the CEO of Ella's Kitchen, shared his experience with vulnerability after the death of his managing director, Cath Empringham, in February 2020, just before the coronavirus pandemic hit. She died suddenly when on holiday. Mark had been a close friend of hers for over ten years, so this came as a massive blow to him and the company.

His first instinct was to get everyone in the business together to tell them but, following the advice of a friend, he realised he couldn't do that. He needed to tell people individually and attend to their needs.

It was his teams' needs that he put before his own. He openly admits that he was still struggling with the issue at the time of interviewing (November 2021). He found that in protecting everyone else and helping them work through their challenges, he had neglected himself. This is something he's actively working on through therapy, a meditation course and ongoing practice, and recently getting a dog. He's keen that he continues to explore this journey for himself.

Mark wanted to share with employees that he was still struggling with Cath's death and this wasn't something that he could easily move on from. He actively stated that he had accessed the free bereavement counselling available through the company and was quite intentional about why he shared this. He hoped that, through his openness, others might seek this route too.

As a result, he noticed that people came to him more actively to talk and have a walk. On those walks, they would open up about their struggles. What he'd enabled, quite unintentionally, was greater connection with some of his staff. They related to each other's difficulties and shared the same pain.

Mark told me after the interview that his wife had always said, 'You can't get true connection without vulnerability.' This is what he found out first-hand.

Mark Reynolds, CEO of technology company Hable, experienced something similar with his former managing director, Sean O'Shea. In January 2019, Sean joined Mark, who had been his colleague at Microsoft before going on to set up Hable. Soon after Sean's arrival as managing director, he experienced what he now knows as a relapse into depression.

This was a difficult time for both Sean and Mark. Sean was grappling with the mist and fogginess that depression brings. He described depression as a condition that 'stops you acting the way you want to'.[81] Mark, at the time, didn't know what to do or say and was quite open about this. He just knew he had to protect the business and consequently, both men admit, their initial conversations about what was happening were not as healthy as they could have been.

Mark was open to learning new things and really keen to find a way with Sean that would support him through this period so that he could recover. For his part, Sean took a few practical steps. He took two weeks off and, before he left, wrote the whole company an email entitled 'Me, my head and I'. He explained to colleagues exactly what was happening, how he was struggling and what steps he was taking.

On his return, he reported, the replies to that email were part of his recovery. Sean received an outpouring of not only support from his colleagues, but also openness about other people's mental-health challenges.

Quite early on in her last role as managing director, Helen Gillett shared her mental-health story. I asked her how she balanced the desire to be open with the need to show backbone or strength as a leader. She reported that when she did share her story in a stress awareness week, some members of staff found it deeply uncomfortable. They may have found it hard to hear that when she felt depressed, she struggled to get out of bed at times.

In spite of that, she felt it was important to share. It built a huge amount of trust because she knew others were struggling. She could feel the sense of stress in the business and wanted them to know they were not alone. This opened up conversations around wellbeing in significant ways.

She admitted she needed to balance this with a strong backbone. She is clear she isn't a pushover and still has high expectations for people's performance. Being open doesn't compromise this.

When I asked podcast guest Clair Heaviside, who we met in Chapter 11, what the hardest thing about running her company is, she said, 'Coming to work every day and keeping going.'[82] As an entrepreneur running a small business, she reported that there was a lot coming at her every day. She talked about putting on a 'courage cape' and believing in herself to help her drive through.

Clair came to a well-formed conclusion about her journey. She said she had to 'go through a lot of shit, then come out the other side and look back and accept what [I'd] gone through and feel confident and calm about the place [I'd] arrived at'.[83] The tough stuff has made her who she is today and helped her connect with staff more deeply. She's suffered post-traumatic stress disorder (PTSD) through some violent incidents and been through a divorce, so she needed to develop a narrative around this that meant she could feel stronger.

This reminds me of a quote by Michelle Obama: 'You should never view your challenges as a disadvantage. Instead, it's important for you to understand that your experience facing and overcoming adversity is actually one of your biggest advantages.'[84] This kind of reframing points to the active way Clair manages herself, which we looked at earlier in the book.

Clair says that her past pushed her to the absolute brink of suffering. Through that, she has created a lot of clarity. On the wall in Serotonin's office in Manchester is 'Good things come to those who create', a phrase that she wrote down to represent the business's driven movement through adversity to creativity. There is an inherent optimism in the work at Serotonin – I guess the clue is in the name. Clair is open about her journey and bringing people with her, role modelling in a way that is quite profound.

Grace Francis, chief experience officer at Accenture Song, is someone who actively lets people in. I mentioned previously the way Grace encourages conversation around their nonbinary gender. They are keen for people to know about it and witness how it helps others feel more comfortable with the ways in which they themselves feel different.

Another key way they let people in is simply via deep relationships with their colleagues on a one-to-one basis. Grace mentioned a group setting in which someone talked about going through a tough IVF journey and another person shared that they'd recently had a miscarriage – a palpable moment of human connection between colleagues. Powerful stuff.

Grace said that this kind of connection is partly built through people sharing vulnerability one-to-one, being open about themselves and not being fearful of what happens next. Many leaders are fearful of saying or doing the wrong thing, so they pull away from intimacy in business relationships. Grace tells their colleagues, 'Nothing is too much. I'm not scared or worried, just tell me what you need to tell me.'[85]

For the first time in my life, I witnessed a solid sense of that attitude with my first coach. I had come to her off the back of being extremely down and anxious; I had been off work for about six weeks having left my previous employer without working my notice period because of how dangerous the environment felt. I had tried sleeping tablets and anti-anxiety tablets but given them up because they made me feel terrible.

I couldn't sleep. Lots of people were worried about me and this made me more fearful of my own emotions. When I sat down with my coach Rachel, she looked at me like I had all the capacity in the world. In that moment, something shifted and I started to feel differently about myself.

Letting people in partly means *sharing who you are*, but it also means *hearing people fully*; allowing yourself to be touched by their sadness without being dragged down by it; and knowing that you can hold their emotions without trying to fix them.

These are skills we can hone through experience.

You don't have to dive in head-first; just see how you can hold the strong backbone of your belief in someone else despite their difficulties and know that you don't have to fix them. You are simply there for them. Hold that intention and they will feel it deeply.

Removing the professional mask

Grace Francis is aware that many things are beyond their capacity, so they are really open to talking about things like wider support, therapy or coaching, and being open to their needs in the first instance. Many leaders can fear that once they've opened the Pandora's box of vulnerability, they can't put it away again. Grace thinks leaders need to trust that people can move into different contexts. If they've shown up for work, virtually or face to face, let's trust they can shift gear, and if they can't, we can be there to catch them. Like all things, it will pass.

John Timpson, the chairman of Timpson, thinks it's really important to be open about his mental health. He has experienced depression and says that the most difficult thing about being depressed is thinking that you're alone. Consequently, he's written about it in a mental health at work book and is keen to keep the conversation going.[86]

He says the body has a way of telling us, 'That's enough.' Often people who experience depression are those who place high expectations on themselves. He says Timpson now has a permanent in-house counsellor to support people in a stable way.[87]

Andy Woodfield, the partner at PwC, talked about the dangers of people feeling like they have to be 'a professional' at work. Practically, he said, this can show itself as a mask over the real person. This kind of protective stance usually points to earlier conditioning in either our childhood or work life (mostly both) and the way many of us feel the need to protect ourselves as a result.

The issue with this kind of veneer is that it prevents us really getting to know people and gaining that all-important emotional awareness of how to treat each other. We can't force people to open up, but we can set up systems like Pip Jamieson's randomised coffee catch-ups, which allow more personal connections, or build close one-to-one connections with our team.

This needs to be modelled from the top. We may ask ourselves, 'What could I share that would allow those I lead to get to know me more fully?' This should be neither forced nor a one-off exercise. Instead, it is an intention we can set and allow ourselves to experiment with.

KEY TAKEAWAYS

- Vulnerability can be a polarising word. Everyone is on their own journey.

- Letting people in is about the power of connection that emerges when we share something deep about ourselves or our experiences.

- Opening up doesn't mean we have less backbone; we can still have high expectations.

PRACTICAL WAYS TO LET PEOPLE IN

- Ask yourself, 'How can I share in a way that helps people see my highs and lows?' Hold the question lightly – no immediate answer is required.

- Think about how you can build close one-to-one connections and show your commitment to them as a whole person.

- Allow people to go at their own pace while knowing there is space for their imperfections. You can show this by the way you role model, for example.

- Know that when people share, you don't need to fix them. Hold their experience lightly and show them it isn't too much for you. They will feel your strength and continuous belief in them.

13
Lesson 9: Enact a strong purpose

I have saved this lesson until last as, in many ways, all the others lead up to it.

The truth is that we need to figure out why we are on this planet.

The standout trait I see in the leaders I interviewed for the Conscious Leaders Podcast is the clarity they have about their purpose in life. Some call it a 'calling', others a 'north star', but they all have some clear purpose that orientates their thoughts and actions.

I'm not saying finding your true purpose is easy, nor is it an immediate revelation that happens overnight, but all conscious leaders must be purposeful. They are driven by a deep desire to improve, change and scale their impact. This is backed up by research. McKinsey reports, 'The first distinctive organization-level skill leaders need to develop is the ability to distill a clear, shared and compelling purpose' in conversation with people across the enterprise.[88] Purpose amounts to a clear, shared and compelling aspiration – the north star of the organisation.

What happens when this isn't in place? Podcast guest, Clair Heaviside, said she's worked in places where the vision and purpose of the company were always changing and unclear. This had a really negative impact on wellbeing because, as a result, employees felt they had to constantly re-evaluate where they fitted in and what their value was. This is mental friction that a business needs to avoid.

Understand the why behind your work

One of the most purposeful leaders I have interviewed is Hephzi Pemberton, founder of Equality Group. She believes that having a strong purpose is fundamental to employees connecting to the business, so they can understand and own the why behind their work.

Practically, for Hephzi, this involves her teams collectively reviewing the purpose of the business on an annual basis. She reports that these participatory discussions are hugely motivating for people as they reconnect employees with the bigger picture. It's a reminder of the impact of their day-to-day work.

Beyond that, Hephzi attributes her ability to hone her vision partly to her advisory board and other influential people in her life. She believes that surrounding herself with great people who will help her push her thinking is vital. She also takes regular retreats which provide her with the space and stillness to allow her thinking to evolve.

As an individual, Hephzi divides her purpose into three titles that she is continually working on, namely inclusion innovator, business builder and servant-leader. For her, this is firstly about opening doors and access for those who don't usually have a seat at the table, secondly about being creative and commercial as an entrepreneur and thirdly, how she seeks to be a leader, which, as she puts it, 'puts my own ego aside'.[89] These titles or modes she has given herself are a key way of orientating herself and her role and purpose.

CASE STUDY: ELIMINATING BIAS

EPISODE 3: THE CONSCIOUS LEADERS PODCAST

Someone with a truly inspiring purpose is Daniel Hulme, the CEO of AI company Satalia. Daniel describes his purpose in life and work as scaling his social impact to the size of a planet. It is a clear vision that informs every action Daniel undertakes and is probably the most ambitious one that I have heard yet.

This goes back to the company values we discussed in the introductory chapters. I have observed that Daniel's purpose is embedded in all of his behaviour, just as a company purpose should be fully supported by the underlying values and behaviours of its employees.

One example I saw in the way he leads his employees is his effort to eliminate as much bias as possible from his organisation. This helps him serve his purpose in supporting human dignity, one of his founding principles. One way he does this is altering the way pay increases are decided in his company. He wants employees to proportionally and anonymously vote on the pay increases of their colleagues, reporting that he often isn't the best person to decide someone's pay increase so this should be decided by 'the crowd'.

To simplify, employees are routinely able to judge the pay increases of their colleagues based on an algorithm which determines the weighting of their scores. The algorithm calculates how much these people work with a specific colleague, thus determining the weighting of their opinion on that colleague's salary increase. They are given information about the market rate for the colleague's role to help them make their choice.

An intern at the company could have a larger input into the pay decision than the CEO. This, Daniel has decided, is the fairest way. As human beings, we have biases, and these biases lead us to listen to some people more than others. It might be that we don't see the potential in someone simply because they don't speak the same language as us. This may be no reflection on their ability or potential.

From my perspective, this system at Satalia goes a long way to:

- Allowing those closest and most familiar to a particular employee to anonymously and fairly rate their ability

- Creating a ripple effect, which is less about how much people impress their boss and more about a 360-degree view on their work, reflected in their pay

This points to collective success and shows Daniel's desire to innovate, creating the most humanly dignified workplace he can. He has an active vision. Keep going at this kind of innovation, Daniel! We need this broader thinking to disrupt the systems most of us have in place, which may be propagating negative behaviour.

The other way that Daniel exhibits his purpose is that he doesn't have line managers at the organisation, not in a traditional sense. Each project has 'circle leaders' and people rotate in and out of leadership positions depending on the project. This points to autonomy (Chapter 9) – he wants to create as much autonomy in his company as is humanly possible.

These ideas may seem radical to some (and it is worth noting that Satalia has the expertise in-house to develop the software to facilitate them), but they point to Daniel's purpose and vision. He is keen that we follow the Hippocratic Oath 'First do no harm', along with 'Live beyond yourself', and give as much to our purpose as possible. This way, he's able to translate the company values into real-life practices.

Make values real

I have worked with many company leaders to help ground their values in reality. Sometimes, companies have big, bold words on the wall-like 'quality', 'customer care', 'compassion' as core values, but nobody really remembers them or thinks they are relevant. They're seen as a tick-box exercise.

If we're going to have useful values, then we need people's agreement and buy-in on what they are in the first place. We need to talk about how we know they are playing out in ways that are aligned and meaningful. This translates values into behaviours, actions and policies (where needed).

If our values are indeed meaningful, then our business will have a strong culture. If we have a strong culture, we will be building a strong employer brand, one that attracts and retains great talent. The modern-day workforce is more and more demanding of this kind of realness – they will see through empty values.

Running simple and practical workshops around values and purpose helps us dig deep and get ourselves and our teams more connected and committed to our work. Our company values and purpose may evolve, so we can check in annually with our teams to make sure that they still represent who we are collectively. This is a huge opportunity for everyone to step up and be part of a committed conversation around culture.

Jon Alexander, CEO at New Citizenship Project, talks about being on a mission to see people as citizens instead of consumers and facilitate the organisations he works with to enact this. He asks clients, 'What would it look like to bring the same creative energy [that you put] into selling stuff into involving people [in the cause you are pursuing]?'[90] If you see people as consumers, you're starting from the wrong place. It is then merely about 'How can we sell people stuff?' whereas if you start from a place of seeing them as citizens, you need to ask yourself, 'What are we trying to do in the world? What's the point? Is this work generative of good things for society or potentially destructive?'

Jon has written a whole book on the subject, which I would highly recommend, called *Citizens: Why the key to fixing everything is all of us*. Through his consultancy, he is helping other organisational leaders become more purposeful. Does he receive pushback? Yes at times; he's challenging the status quo and the 'experts' in a business and their purpose. He's getting them to think more deeply about the work they do. For example, he challenged a leader at a council to think about how they address big questions such as 'How can we work with people to make their own places better?' as opposed to just being a service-delivery organisation.

In a recent event I attended in St Neots near Cambridge, UK, he spoke about the use of language. He sees the words 'service-provider' and 'service-user' as detrimental to public bodies as they reduce the dynamic between them and the public to a consumer one. This misses the opportunity for these businesses to engage the public *in* their work, rather than have them treating them as bodies to solve all their problems. Instead, it needs to be a participatory approach.

His work is based on two core beliefs:

- People can and want to contribute to the society that they are in.
- We're fundamentally shaped by the prompts that are around us (which can go against our desire to contribute).

Consumer organisations have a huge role in these prompts. He wants them to be purposeful.

For his clients, to make this practical, he talks about three Ps of purpose, platform and prototype. Purpose is 'What's this organisation doing in the world that is *so* big, it needs people to help us do it?' (as opposed to just selling products). Platform is about 'What structures and processes do we create to make it joyful and meaningful to be part of this purpose?' Prototype is 'How do we build the energy? How do we get that purpose moving?'

Practically, internally in his organisation, Jon says this applies to things like responding to diversity and inclusion more broadly. He and his teams have recognised that they are quite a white organisation and are bringing their own practices to grow in this area, such as group listening and enquiry to explore the subject more deeply. They want to be an actively antiracist organisation and are putting in processes to grow in purposeful ways, both as individuals and as a collective.

Podcast guest Jean Baptiste Oldenhove also has a clear purpose. His work is based on helping drive investment into sustainability, supported by his awareness of people around the world who are suffering. He wants to reduce that suffering, which could be due to lack of education or lack of wealth, which points to a lack of *human* sustainability. Therefore, human sustainability, alongside ecological sustainability, has to be central to any of his projects.

For him personally, it is important to adopt what he calls a 'holistically coherent' mode, which practically means that he's the same person at home as he is at work. He has the same goals in life and is working to realise them across his life. This enables him to point to his true north.

The way to make this possible is to be connected firstly to the ground, secondly to your interests and what feeds your soul, and thirdly to others, including those outside your immediate circles such as other races or religions. This enables you to participate fully in life as well as you can.

KEY TAKEAWAYS

- The best leaders know why they are on the planet – they are working towards a strong and committed purpose that supersedes everything.

- More than ever, employees are demanding a genuine purpose and culture from employers. With that comes a strong employer brand and, subsequently, the ability to attract and retain great people.

PRACTICAL WAYS TO ENACT A STRONG PURPOSE

- Keep asking yourself 'Why?' about the work you are doing. 'What's the real reason behind this? What's the point? How does this support our world?' Hone your calling or north star.

- Involve employees in this conversation. Allow them to:

  - Build or hone your values

  - Describe and decide how they play out realistically in terms of day-to-day behaviours, practices and policies

- Revisit your purpose yearly with your teams, even if it's just for a quick check-in.

Conclusion: Leader as facilitator and coach

As I draw this book to a close, I hope that the leaders' stories, my own experiences and the global research I've presented have given you practical insights into what makes truly great leaders who stand out from the crowd. It may be impressive, but great leadership is built on simple practices and behaviours. To conclude our journey, I will bring all this together in terms of what the mode of a leader needs to be in our modern world and discuss how you can integrate what most interests you into your day-to-day life.

What this amounts to is a new kind of role for a leader – one that is both visionary, ordinary and relational. This type of leadership enables others and, in turn, the impact that you can have as a leader. The scale of the societal challenges and opportunities we all face is so great, we need leaders who can take it to the next level.

The evolution of leadership

The hallmarks of a successful leader have changed dramatically over the years. At the turn of the twentieth century, people thought that a leader was born, not made. Either you had what you needed to be a successful leader in your lineage or you didn't.

As the twentieth century progressed, it became apparent that the traits of a leader could be learnt and there were behaviours that represented what made a successful leader. As we entered the 1990s, we saw leaders in technology like Bill Gates and Steve Jobs on stage. There was a heroism about them as they revealed their latest tech gadget to rapturous applause. People followed their every move, monitored their every word and worshipped their presence. These leaders were uber-visionary in style.

What we see in a successful leader today is a much more ordinary and relational nature. They have a vision, but are down to earth and open. In the modern world, information is everywhere. Anyone can become an expert in practically anything from the comfort of their own bedroom, so leadership is less about information and control, and more about the traits shown by the Conscious Leaders Podcast guests.

These leaders are focused on creating connections between people through great intention, listening and purpose. They want a work environment to be a place of belonging, allowing people to see their own biases through leaning into difficult conversations. Importantly, these leaders develop all this from a core place of self-management. They recognise that the work starts with themselves.

John Hesler, my first podcast guest, shared how the process of helping people, reasoning with them, allowing them to go on their own journey, *does* take longer than the traditional directive style of leading. It's quicker to say, 'You're just doing this because of x', but as he explained, 'You'll get your point across in this way, but it won't stick.'[91] People need the chance to be able to come to their own conclusions so they can really learn.

In the past, particularly in the pre-internet age, the world was much more structured. This meant that a controlling type of leadership worked. We could plan specific things and work towards them in a linear fashion. Traditional operationally driven top-down leadership could be effective.

Nowadays, the world is highly unpredictable and uncertain. This means we need to facilitate an environment where that uncertainty is considered normal. We need to work together and use all of our knowledge and collaboration skills to navigate it.

For this to happen, we need to get the best out of people. We need to recognise that we've all come from mildly to considerably complicated histories, but that – with a bit of willingness, and a whole lot of facilitation and coaching from us as leaders – everyone can get out of their own way and enact their own strengths and purpose through their work.

This truly meaningful work starts with you as leader and your own behaviour, as exemplified through the podcast guests. Perhaps you will have other traits or behaviours that work as effectively for you. To me, this work is a conversation in itself. I'll be reviewing the podcast content as I continue to delve into the minds of great leaders and what helps take their work to the next level.

The modern workforce

The other major change in leadership context is the motivational factors of the workforce. We used to have employees who, put simply, could be told what to do. Whether they were factory or call-centre workers, people had predictable job instructions that they needed to follow to the letter.

Nowadays, these jobs are becoming fewer – mostly through the evolution of technology as such roles tend to be taken by automated systems. People now expect to be much more empowered.

The modern workforce demands more meaning and purpose at work. Employees have a psychological contract in their heads that expects a strong culture to enable and empower them. Company leaders need to be much more aware of their employer brand, so that people see the unique opportunities they can reap from working and staying with them.

Now people are much more empowered at work, they often disagree. Diversity of thought is a good thing and should be encouraged, but it needs skilful navigation so that it is generative of strong relationships. We as leaders can't just hire diverse teams; we need them to work together effectively.

Andy Woodfield spoke about hiring a diverse team being the easy bit; getting people to work together, on the other hand, was mayhem at first. 'It would have been much easier to hire a bunch of straight white blokes,'[92] he told me, but Andy has a passion for inclusive practices and embraces difference as part of the growth of the team. He has found that most of the root causes of issues in his leadership teams are people not really listening to or understanding each other. All he does is facilitate their reconnection so they can understand each other's perspective.

He breaks this down in his podcast episode. A big problem can actually become quite trivial when people get together in a room to talk about it. McKinsey reports, 'Leaders must create space for real listening, foster creative collision of perspectives, and make sure every voice is heard, not for consensus, but to take perspective and to ensure true diversity.'[93] Inclusion is not only a great thing for us to do for its own sake, it's also how McKinsey sees modern organisations growing effectively.

Often, leaders are keen to skip past the disagreements and the rumblings and get on with the 'real' work.

I'm keen to champion the fact that moments of challenge *are* the real work. They are an opportunity to see different perspectives, work through differences to find common ground and learn more about people. It is in these moments that we develop our emotional awareness that Google's Project Aristotle highlighted as such a key factor in a team's success. This is where we connect as human beings.

Many of us just want to get through the difficult stuff so that we can finally be calm, but we now live in a business world where turbulence and uncertainty are here to stay. The reactive mindsets of scarcity, authority and certainty no longer fit the ever-changing world. McKinsey tells us that they cause us to focus inward and backward and lose sight of amazing opportunities.[94]

One approach, which a few of the leaders I interviewed show clearly, that is core to our development is continuous improvement. My youngest inter-viewee, Bejay Mulenga, CEO of Supa Network (who was only twenty-five at the time of interviewing), has a wise approach. He talks about continually chipping away at goals, revisiting them every day in a way that is meaningful. We can enjoy this journey if we frame it with steadiness and purpose.

Conscious leadership as a journey

It is all too easy to put pressure on ourselves to sud-denly become the leader we want to be. What my podcast guests and my wider coaching and facilita-tion work have taught me is that yes, there are big traits, behaviours and philosophies that we can aim for, but this is a journey that we can work on every day. It is a journey made up of simple habits and prac-tices which create change over the long term.

One key area that leaders tend to neglect is their own wellbeing. They are driven, which is fantastic, but they can sacrifice themselves. I did this to myself and I paid the price: I experienced anxiety and depression on and off for many years and it was tough.

Sometimes, we end up with an over-inflated view of our own importance and indispensability. At times, there are consequences of this as we struggle to look after ourselves and delegate effectively. Our own emotional state needs to be a priority because without it, we will not have the capacity to support and facilitate others.

If you have a small team, you may be the only leader, but if you have other leaders around you, you will be able to influence them to grow their facilitatory leadership style too. This will take some of the weight off you.

I always finish my podcast interviews by asking guests how they look after themselves. Often, they report that they don't do enough on this front; some are better than others. Bejay Mulenga is my strongest podcast guest so far for prioritising his own wellbeing through his 'no meetings before 10am' rule, regular bike rides and a tight nutrition regime. This gives him the headspace to continually step back, review and re-evaluate his focus. John Hesler with his twice daily meditation shows a routine dedicated to stillness and poise. He has experienced adrenal burnout and his own awakening as a result, so he doesn't see any alternative to being disciplined about his own headspace.

I have encouraged this before, but I want to emphasise that your own active reflective spaces are important. This space could be shared with a peer group, a coach or another who helps you evolve as a human being and a leader. Sometimes, simple accountability with another leader can help you, but set up the environment to be one of challenge and support. There is no point talking to someone who will just agree with you – you need someone who will hold you to account and know when to be hard and soft with you so you can reflect on your own behaviour and grow as a result.

This work starts with you. As you develop in this way, leaders who work with you (if you have the privilege of a leadership team) will be able to take on conscious leadership practices too. Who knows? Maybe others will adapt more naturally to this style and teach you new things about how to behave.

Becoming a manager/leader – however you want to put it – comes with responsibility. This is not an opportunity for egos, but to serve and facilitate. Taking other leaders on this journey with you is important. You must show the humility of your own journey, your highs and lows, to help people see your human side. It will help them recognise what could be possible for them.

Perhaps the conscious leadership concepts we've covered in this book feel possible to you and there is a lot you want to try, or perhaps it all feels like too much. In this case, changing something small is a good place to start. This could be about the way you practise listening or taking a short pause or meditation each morning before launching into the day.

We need to hold this journey lightly so that it doesn't become a burden in itself. Otherwise, we treat self-development as one more thing on the to-do list. For me, I revisit my question 'How do I live my life with more ease and fun?' This usually helps support my journey.

Systems and identity

For conscious leadership to take effect easily, we need to create habits and systems to make it happen. Depending on your personality type, you could have a monthly call or WhatsApp dialogue with your peer group or another leader who can hold you accountable on this subject. If you like lists, you might benefit from making a record of each time you have let someone else take a decision and reward yourself when you hit a certain number.

If you want support to make a quick but significant change, a professional coach will help you in this transition. Find a coach who works for you – you might speak to a few who come recommended to find the one who speaks your language. Your potential relationship with them is key. You will want to build a high degree of trust so that they can support you fully and challenge you to overcome barriers. Whatever else, you need a system that works for you.

James Clear, who focuses on continuous improvement in habits and decision making, says in his book *Atomic Habits* that getting 1% or 2% better each day amounts to a huge improvement over the long term.[95] Thus, starting small can help.

'You do not rise to the level of your goals,' he tells us. 'You fall to the level of your systems.' These goals will be dreams without systems to support them, so it is all about the types of habits that motivate you. Find out what system you need in your life, eg a coach, accountability buddy, peer group etc, to adapt your routines to make the change you want.

James also talks about how you self-identify, which is a significant starting point. To apply his rationale, you need a positive dialogue around identity. For example, you could try, 'I am a progressive leader who gives away power and facilitates others' decision making.' From here, you can make the change.

See what it's like to identify with this or whatever words resonate with you. Then you can start to live the words of the person you want to be. James Clear talks about two steps:[96]

- Decide the type of person you want to be

- Prove it to yourself with small wins

I have found this to be one of the most empowering things I have read because it has allowed me to overcome identities I played on repeat for many years. These were identities such as 'I am a worrier' or 'I am an anxious person'. If this pops up for me now, I gently put it down. I don't need that identity anymore and I can focus on being calm, collaborative and productive. This will only happen with the right habits and systems to support me such as exercise, my coach and a daily meditation practice.

Summing up

If I were to sum up my work around the next level of leadership, it's about daily conversations – ones with ourselves, our teams and in groups to facilitate understanding and change. In this way, we enable the continuous improvement we seek. In doing so, we work through difficult things, while maintaining an openness to be wrong or to change.

To quote world-renowned authorities on adult learning and development, Robert Kegan and Lisa Laskow Lahey, 'Every meeting and encounter is simultaneously an opportunity to work on learning goals, pursue business excellence, and help people become more capable versions of themselves.'[97] In other words, these encounters are an opportunity to step up to next level leadership.

A gardener creates the right environment for things to grow. Of course, the weather can be windy or stormy, but if the people we nurture are able to develop strong roots, they are likely to grow. Some will grow unexpectedly, some may wilt, but if like the gardner, we keep up the steady work in the general environment, overall, people will flourish.

Throughout this book, I have concentrated on how we *are* as a leader, how we show up. This amalgamates many of the traits I have shared. This is about the energy we give out – our intention; our purpose;

CONCLUSION: LEADER AS FACILITATOR AND COACH

the way we listen; the way we delegate and create a space of safety and belonging. It's about translating how we feel into reality. To do so, we may need to hone our feelings and deepen our thinking and beliefs for the benefit of others and our wider purpose.

This is what it means to take our leadership to the next level

---

That's why I encourage you to work on things like your positive intent. Getting really clear about your belief in people and your intention, and linking that all the way through to the purpose you have on this planet, is the journey I have taken you on in this book. As you work on these things, you will feel more aligned and your strength of conscious behaviour will bring you deeper confidence and belief in yourself. I know this because I've worked for seven years with leaders on their paths and I never underestimate the immense potential of this work. When it's balanced with your personal life, I would argue there is no greater work.

I'm sure you will have come to this book with good intentions and seeds of thought around how you want to grow and change. I encourage you to dip into the chapters again. Revisit the content to see where you would like to focus personally.

I like to visualise our actualisation as leaders and human beings as concentric circles. If we all sit in the middle just thinking about ourselves as individuals, we are basically screwed as a human race. If we can think outside ourselves to our family, community, employees, and then wider to humanity and the planet, we give ourselves a chance as a species to make this world better.

I'll leave you with this question:

What's your next level on this path?

I invite you to take it.

I wish you well on your journey forward.

The Conscious Leaders Podcast guests

Episode 1: John Hesler, founder, Napkin Group

Episode 2: June Cory, founder, My Mustard

Episode 3: Daniel Hulme, CEO, Satalia

Episode 4: Tom Tapper, co-founder and CEO, Nice and Serious

Episode 5: Helen Gillett, COO, BetterSpace (Former MD, Affinity for Business at the time of interviewing)

Episode 6: Andy Woodfield, PwC partner and author, *This Is Your Moment*[98]

Episode 7: Ciaron Dunne, CEO, Genie Ventures

Episode 8: Shanice Mears, co-founder, The Elephant Room

Episode 9: Jon Alexander, CEO, New Citizenship Project and author, *Citizens*[99]

Episode 10: Pip Jamieson, founder and CEO, The Dots

Episode 11: 2020 Highlights

Episode 12: Hephzi Pemberton, founder and CEO, Equality Group and author, *The Diversity Playbook*[100]

Episode 13: Jean Baptiste Oldenhove, founder and CEO, EstariGroup

Episode 14: Steve O'Brien, founder and CEO, Newicon

Episode 15: Guy Singh-Watson, founder, Riverford

Episode 16: Phil Wild, CEO, James Cropper

Episode 17: Nicole Sadd, CEO, Rothamsted Enterprises

Episode 18: Charlotte Williams, CEO, SevenSix

Episode 19: Susan Glenholme, managing partner, Debenhams Ottaway

Episode 20: Bejay Mulenga, founder, Supa Network

Episode 21: Cheryl Luzet, CEO, Wagada

Episode 22: Mark Cuddigan, CEO, Ella's Kitchen

Episode 23: 2021 Highlights Episode

Episode 24: Grace Francis, global chief creative and design officer, WONGDOODY (chief experience officer at Accenture Song at the time of interviewing)

Episode 25: Lee Timbrell, general manager, Vision Labs (owned by Specsavers)

Episode 26: Clair Heaviside, co-founder, Serotonin

Episode 27: Sir John Timpson CBE, chairman, Timpson

New episodes are released each month – visit www.consciousleaders.org.uk/podcast to listen, or search for 'Conscious Leaders Podcast with Ruth Farenga'

Notes

1. Ruth Farenga, *Emotional Intelligence: Connecting at work* (Conscious Leaders, 2019), www.consciousleaders.org.uk/ blog/emotional-intelligence-connecting-at-work, accessed August 2022
2. M Schwantes, 'Why are your employees quitting?' (23 October 2017), www.inc.com/marcel-schwantes/why-are-your-employees-quitting-a-study-says-it-comes-down-to-any-of-these-6-reasons.html, accessed 20 September 2021
3. B Holland, 'Bringing out the best in people: An interview with Warren Bennis' (30 May 2012), https:// thesystemsthinker.com/bringing-out-the-best-in-people-an-interview-with-warren-bennis, accessed 22 September 2021
4. DH Pink, *Drive: The surprising truth about what motivates us* (Canongate, 2009)
5. G Singh-Watson, 'Episode 15: Becoming an employee-owned business', The Conscious Leaders Podcast (2022), www.consciousleaders.org.uk/podcast, accessed July 2022
6. G Smith, 'Employee retention: The real cost of losing an employee' (17 September 2021), www.peoplekeep.com/ blog/employee-retention-the-real-cost-of-losing-an-employee, accessed 10 October 2021

7. Personal communication
8. CIPD, 'The psychological contract' (9 February 2022), www.cipd.co.uk/knowledge/fundamentals/relations/employees/psychological-factsheet#gref, accessed 10 March 2022
9. Personal communication
10. Personal communication
11. Personal communication
12. The National Trust, 'Latest statement on reopening and coronavirus' (5 March 2020), www.nationaltrust.org.uk/press-release/the-national-trusts-latest-statement-on-coronavirus-covid-19, accessed 20 October 2021
13. BPS, *Total Immersion: Resourcing that Lives and Breathes the Brand* (January 2017), https://onyxcomms.com/wp-content/uploads/2017/01/bps-total-immersion-white-paper1.pdf, accessed 20 October 2021
14. Ruth Farenga, *Emotional Intelligence: Connecting at work* (Conscious Leaders, 2019), www.consciousleaders.org.uk/blog/emotional-intelligence-connecting-at-work, accessed August 2022
15. G Singh-Watson, 'Episode 15: Becoming an employee-owned business', The Conscious Leaders Podcast (2022), www.consciousleaders.org.uk/podcast, accessed July 2022
16. P Dolan, 'Five minutes with Paul Dolan: "Happiness is experiences of pleasure and purpose over time"', LSE blog (28 August 2015), https://blogs.lse.ac.uk/politicsandpolicy/five-minutes-with-paul-dolan/, accessed August 2022
17. D Goleman, *Emotional Intelligence: Why it can matter more than IQ* (Random House, 2012)
18. A Toren, 'Are you emotionally intelligent? It'll help you rise above failure', NBC News (February 2014), www.nbcnews.com/id/wbna54531766, accessed January 2022
19. D Goleman, 'What makes a leader?', *Harvard Business Review* (January 2004), https://hbr.org/2004/01/what-makes-a-leader, accessed August 2022
20. As quoted in Jennifer Siebel Newsom, 'Miss representation' (2011), Sundance Film Festival documentary
21. K Racovolis, 'The next LinkedIn? This woman is connecting 1 million creatives to jobs', *Forbes* (18 July 2016), www.forbes.com/sites/kateracovolis/2016/07/18/the-next-linkedin-this-woman-is-connecting-1-million-creatives-to-jobs/, accessed August 2022

22. K Scott, *Radical Candor: How to get what you want by saying what you mean* (Macmillan, 2019 revised edition) p xii
23. M Reitz, 'How your power silences truth' (2017), www.youtube.com/watch?v=Sq475Us1KXg, accessed 27 October 2021
24. N Kline, *Time to Think: Listening to ignite the human mind* (Cassell Orion, 1999) pp 62–63
25. Personal communication
26. D Goleman and RE Boyatzis, 'Social intelligence and the biology of leadership', *Harvard Business Review* (September 2008), https://hbr.org/2008/09/social-intelligence-and-the-biology-of-leadership, accessed September 2021
27. M Williams and D Penman, *Mindfulness: Finding peace in a frantic world* (Piatkus, 2011)
28. B Hölzel, J Carmody, M Vangel, C Congleton, SM Yerramsetti, T Gard and SW Lazar, 'Mindfulness practice leads to increases in regional brain gray matter density', *Psychiatry Research: Neuroimaging*, 19/1 (2011), 36–43, www.ncbi.nlm.nih.gov/pmc/articles/PMC3004979, accessed 10 January 2022
29. M Reitz and M Chaskalson, 'Mindfulness works but only if you work at it', *Harvard Business Review* (4 November 2016), https://hbr.org/2016/11/mindfulness-works-but-only-if-you-work-at-it?autocomplete=true, accessed 10 January 2022
30. Personal communication
31. SR Covey, *The 7 Habits of Highly Effective People: Powerful lessons in personal change interactive edition* (Mango Media Inc, 2016) p 298
32. N Kline, *Time to Think: Listening to ignite the human mind* (Cassell Orion, 1999) p 36
33. K Basman, 'On craving & aversion: The two hindrances to mindful living', The Kula Collective (2019), www.thekulacollective.com/blog-/craving-and-aversion-mindful-living, accessed August 2022
34. J Cory, 'Episode 2: Undeniable positivity and celebrating individuality', The Conscious Leaders Podcast (2022), www.consciousleaders.org.uk/podcast, accessed July 2022
35. Mindtools, 'The Conscious Competence Ladder', www.mindtools.com/pages/article/newISS_96.htm, accessed October 2021

36. American Psychological Association, *Dictionary of Psychology*, 'Empathy', https://dictionary.apa.org/empathy, accessed 30 January 2021

37. D Goleman, 'The focused leader', *Harvard Business Review* (December 2013), https://hbr.org/2013/12/the-focused-leader, accessed 30 January 2022

38. BusinessSolver, '2019 state of workplace empathy' (2019), https://info.businesssolver.com/empathy-2019-executive-summary, accessed August 2022

39. N Kline, *Time to Think: Listening to ignite the human mind* (Cassell Orion, 1999) pp 74–75

40. Personal communication

41. A Woodfield, 'Episode 6: Drop your guard and show us who you really are', The Conscious Leaders Podcast (2022), www.consciousleaders.org.uk/podcast, accessed July 2022

42. C Kininmonth, 'Brené Brown: 4 reasons being unclear is unkind', The Growth Faculty (2 March 2019), www.thegrowthfaculty.com/blog/BrenBrown4reasonsbeingUnclearisUnkind, accessed July 2022

43. P Wild, 'Episode 16: A forward thinking, responsible and caring business', The Conscious Leaders Podcast (2022), www.consciousleaders.org.uk/podcast, accessed July 2022

44. C Dunne, 'Episode 7: A start-up mentality in a medium-sized business', The Conscious Leaders Podcast (2022), www.consciousleaders.org.uk/podcast, accessed July 2022

45. DH Pink, *Drive: The surprising truth about what motivates us* (Canongate, 2009)

46. J Timpson, 'Episode 27: Upside down management', The Conscious Leaders Podcast (2022), www.consciousleaders.org.uk/podcast, accessed July 2022

47. J Hesler, 'Episode 1: Finding his way and releasing control', The Conscious Leaders Podcast (2022), www.consciousleaders.org.uk/podcast, accessed July 2022

48. www.quoteslyfe.com/quote/We-are-at-our-most-powerful-the-28404, accessed August 2022

49. S O'Brien, 'Episode 14: The game of people', The Conscious Leaders Podcast (2022), www.consciousleaders.org.uk/podcast, accessed July 2022

50. R Lowe 'How Netflix leads the way in HR', Undercover Recruiter (No date), https://theundercoverrecruiter.com/netflix-company-hr/, accessed August 2022

51. S O'Brien, 'Episode 14: The game of people', The Conscious Leaders Podcast (2022), www.consciousleaders.org.uk/podcast, accessed July 2022

52. C Gallo, 'Steve Jobs demanded fearless feedback and so should you', Inc. (No date), www.inc.com/carmine-gallo/steve-jobs-demanded-fearless-feedback-and-so-should-you.html, accessed August 2022

53. S O'Brien, 'Episode 14: The game of people', The Conscious Leaders Podcast (2022), www.consciousleaders.org.uk/podcast, accessed July 2022

54. D Hulme, 'Episode 3: Scaling social impact to the size of a planet', The Conscious Leaders Podcast (2022), www.consciousleaders.org.uk/podcast, accessed July 2022

55. C Williams, 'Episode 18: Challenging a non-inclusive world', The Conscious Leaders Podcast (2022), www.consciousleaders.org.uk/podcast, accessed July 2022

56. J Cory, 'Episode 2: Undeniable positivity and celebrating individuality', The Conscious Leaders Podcast (2022), www.consciousleaders.org.uk/podcast, accessed July 2022

57. S Glenholme, 'Episode 19: Subtle leadership', The Conscious Leaders Podcast (2022), www.consciousleaders.org.uk/podcast, accessed July 2022

58. S Glenholme, 'Episode 19: Subtle leadership', The Conscious Leaders Podcast (2022), www.consciousleaders.org.uk/podcast, accessed July 2022

59. G Francis, 'Episode 24: Radical inclusivity', The Conscious Leaders Podcast (2022), www.consciousleaders.org.uk/podcast, accessed July 2022

60. re:Work, 'Guide: Understand team effectiveness', https://rework.withgoogle.com/guides/understanding-team-effectiveness/steps/introduction/, accessed August 2022

61. N Kline, *Time to Think: Listening to ignite the human mind* (Cassell Orion, 1999) pp 102–103

62. M Reitz and J Higgins, *Speak Up: Say what needs to be said and hear what needs to be heard* (Pearson Education, 2019)

63. M Reitz and J Higgins, *Speak Up: Say what needs to be said and hear what needs to be heard* (Pearson Education, 2019) p 52

64. M Reitz, 'How your power silences truth' (2017), www.youtube.com/watch?v=Sq475Us1KXg, accessed 27 October 2021

65. G Orwell, *Animal Farm* (Reprinted, Penguin Classics, 2000) p 134

66. RK Greenleaf Center for Servant Leadership, 'What is servant leadership?', www.greenleaf.org/what-is-servant-leadership/, accessed January 2022

67. H Gillett, 'Episode 5: A strong backbone and a warm heart', The Conscious Leaders Podcast (2022), www.consciousleaders.org.uk/podcast, accessed July 2022

68. H Gillett, 'Episode 5: A strong backbone and a warm heart', The Conscious Leaders Podcast (2022), www.consciousleaders.org.uk/podcast, accessed July 2022

69. Personal communication

70. H Pemberton, 'Episode 12: Business purpose and focus', The Conscious Leaders Podcast (2022), www.consciousleaders.org.uk/podcast, accessed July 2022

71. H Pemberton, *The Diversity Playbook: Transforming business with inclusion and innovation* (Serapis Bey Publishers, 2021)

72. B Hölzel, J Carmody, M Vangel, C Congleton, SM Yerramsetti, T Gard and SW Lazar, *Psychiatry Research: Neuroimaging*, 19/1 (2011), 36–43, www.ncbi.nlm.nih.gov/pmc/articles/PMC3004979, accessed 10 January 2022

73. S McGreevey, 'Eight weeks to a better brain', *The Harvard Gazette* (21 January 2011), https://news.harvard.edu/gazette/story/2011/01/eight-weeks-to-a-better-brain/, accessed 10 January 2022

74. D Brownlee, 'Doing this at least 10 minutes a day could transform your productivity', *Forbes* (15 January 2020), www.forbes.com/sites/danabrownlee/2020/01/15/doing-this-at-least-10-minutes-a-day-could-transform-your-productivity/?sh=500f4520361d, accessed 11 January 2022

75. Personal communication

76. Personal communication

77. B Horowitz 'What you do is who you are: Lessons from Silicon Valley, Andy Grove, Genghis Khan, slave revolutions and more', The Tim Ferriss Show (2019), https://tim.blog/2019/10/24/ben-horowitz/, accessed August 2022

78. B Horowitz, *What You Do Is Who You Are: How to create your business culture* (William Collins, 2019)

79. G Francis, 'Episode 24: Radical inclusivity', The Conscious Leaders Podcast (2022), www.consciousleaders.org.uk/podcast, accessed July 2022

80. G Francis, 'Episode 24: Radical inclusivity', The Conscious Leaders Podcast (2022), www.consciousleaders.org.uk/podcast, accessed July 2022

81. Personal communication
82. C Heaviside, 'Episode 26: Hacking into trust', The Conscious Leaders Podcast (2022), www.consciousleaders. org.uk/podcast, accessed July 2022
83. C Heaviside, 'Episode 26: Hacking into trust', The Conscious Leaders Podcast (2022), www.consciousleaders. org.uk/podcast, accessed July 2022
84. M Obama, City College of New York commencement speech (2016)
85. G Francis, 'Episode 24: Radical inclusivity', The Conscious Leaders Podcast (2022), www.consciousleaders.org.uk/ podcast, accessed July 2022
86. J Timpson, 'Episode 27: Upside down management', The Conscious Leaders Podcast (2022), www.consciousleaders. org.uk/podcast, accessed July 2022
87. J Timpson, 'Episode 27: Upside down management', The Conscious Leaders Podcast (2022), www.consciousleaders. org.uk/podcast, accessed July 2022
88. McKinsey, 'Leading agile transformation: The new capabilities leaders need to build 21st-century organizations' (October 2018) p 1, https://www.mckinsey. com/business-functions/people-and-organizational-performance/our-insights/leading-agile-transformation-the-new-capabilities-leaders-need-to-build-21st-century-organizations, accessed 14 February 2022
89. Personal communication
90. J Alexander, 'Episode 9: People as citizens, not just consumers', The Conscious Leaders Podcast (2022), www. consciousleaders.org.uk/podcast, accessed July 2022
91. Personal communication
92. A Woodfield, 'Episode 6: Drop your guard and show us who you really are', The Conscious Leaders Podcast (2022), www.consciousleaders.org.uk/podcast, accessed July 2022
93. McKinsey, 'Leading agile transformation: The new capabilities leaders need to build 21st-century organizations' (October 2018), https://www.mckinsey. com/business-functions/people-and-organizational-performance/our-insights/leading-agile-transformation-the-new-capabilities-leaders-need-to-build-21st-century-organizations, accessed 14 February 2022
94. McKinsey, 'Leading agile transformation: The new capabilities leaders need to build 21st-century

organizations' (October 2018), https://www.mckinsey.com/business-functions/people-and-organizational-performance/our-insights/leading-agile-transformation-the-new-capabilities-leaders-need-to-build-21st-century-organizations, accessed 14 February 2022

95. J Clear, *Atomic Habits: Tiny changes, remarkable results* (Penguin Random House, 2018)

96. J Clear, *Atomic Habits: Tiny changes, remarkable results* (Penguin Random House, 2018)

97. R Kegan and LL Lahey, *An Everyone Culture: Becoming a deliberately developmental organization* (Harvard Business School Press, 2016)

98. A Woodfield, *This Is Your Moment: Find and follow your unique path in life and your business* (Panoma, 2021)

99. J Alexander, *Citizens: Why the key to fixing everything is all of us* (Canbury Press, 2022)

100. H Pemberton, *The Diversity Playbook: Transforming business with inclusion and innovation* (Serapis Bey Publishers, 2021)

Further reading

These books have been formative to my development. I hope you enjoy them as much as I have.

Alexander, J, *Citizens: Why the key to fixing everything is all of us* (Canbury Press, 2022)

Berkun, S, *The Year Without Pants: Wordpress.com and the future of work* (Jossey-Bass, 2013)

Clear, J, *Atomic Habits: Tiny habits, remarkable results* (Random House, 2018)

Harris, D, *Meditation for Fidgety Skeptics: A 10% happier how-to book* (Spiegel & Grau, 2017)

Kline, N, *Time to Think: Listening to ignite the human mind* (Cassell Orion, 1999)

Nhat Hanh, T, *Silence: The power of quiet in a world full of noise* (Random House, 2015)

Pink, DH, *Drive: The surprising truth about what motivates us* (Canongate Books, 2009)

Scott, K, *Radical Candor: How to get what you want by saying what you mean* (Macmillan, 2019 revised edition)

Williams, M and Penman, D, *Mindfulness: Finding peace in a frantic world* (Piatkus, 2011)

Acknowledgements

Thank you to my partner Becky for encouraging me to take leaps and realise my dreams – this book is very much part of that. At work, I watch you be a generous people leader who commits to continuously protecting and supporting people. So many benefit from the ripple effect that you create.

The Conscious Leaders Podcast guests have all been instrumental to this work with their honest stories. I have been energised, moved and changed by our conversations and they will always be a part of me. Thanks to those with whom I have had follow-up conversations so that I could dig deeper into our themes. You are all busy, but yet you made space.

I would particularly like to thank Andy Woodfield, for championing me and suggesting I write a book in the first place, and Grace Francis for their huge support around the design and launch of the book.

Thank you so much to the draft book reviewers for all your comments and questions – Andy Woodfield, Ann Hawkins, Annette Jensen, Ciaron Dunne, Helen Gillett, June Cory, Mark Reynolds, Becky Parslow, Rosie Anderson and Paul Edwards. Your feedback has been invaluable.

I'd like to thank the coaches I've had over the years who have helped me become more the person I want to be, namely Rachel Brushfield, Jennifer Clamp and my current coach Fi MacMillan. My coach training was undertaken with Damion Wonfor, founder, Catalyst 14, who provided a mindful and fulfilling space for me and the other trainees to grow as coaches.

Thank you to my therapist Nick Heap for being the wisest and most compassionate person I know. You've been with me at the darkest times and I don't know how I would have got through them without you.

Thank you to the people I work closely with. Firstly, to Jessica Evans, who has been by my side for two years in operations, my podcast producer, Rob Birnie, and to my co-facilitators and fellow coaches, Phil Walsh, Laura Sly and Esme Butterfield. I learn so much in your presence.

Last but not least, I would like to thank my parents who have trusted me to follow my ambitions (including extra thanks to my mum who has done a spot of extra proofreading). You are both so kind – thank you for listening and being so supportive of me on the journey.

The Author

Ruth Farenga is a facilitator, executive coach and speaker. She is founder of Conscious Leaders, a consultancy helping ambitious leaders in technology build a calm, collaborative and productive workplace.

Ruth helps people connect more to themselves, each other and their wider purpose so they can drive both individual and collective success, whatever that means to them. She has worked in corporations such as Pearson Education, Intel Corporation and as a consultant for the WISE Campaign, as well as in a variety of roles spanning sales, training, events and programme management.

In 2019, Ruth started the Conscious Leaders Podcast, on which she showcases great people leaders: CEOs and founders who really step up for their employees. Together, they unpack what's really going on to help listeners understand new philosophies and give practical, actionable takeaways.

She has a diploma in mindfulness teaching, a diploma in transformational coaching accredited by the European Mentoring and Coaching Council (EMCC), and takes regular supervision and silent retreats for her own development.

Ruth loves nature, craft beer and travels with her partner, Becky, and husky, Juno. You can connect with Ruth via:

🌐 www.consciousleaders.org.uk

in www.linkedin.com/in/ruthfarenga

🐦 @RuthFarenga